Ninja Air Fryer Delights Cookbook

Master Your Kitchen in 1200 Days: Affordable, Quick, and Easy Culinary Adventures for Beginners – Bake, Air Fry, Boil, Grill, Roast, Dehydrate Delightfully + 30days meal plan

Thomas N. Smith

All right reserved. No part of this publication may be reproduced, distributed, or transmitted in any form or by any means, including photo copying, recording, or other electronic or mechanical methods, without the prior written permission of the publisher, except in the case of brief quotations embodied in critical reviews and certain other non commercial uses permitted by copyright law.

Copyright © (Thomas N. Smith) (2023)

Table of contents

INTRODUCTION..26
    Brief Overview of the Ninja Air Fryer...................... 27
    How This Cookbook Will Transform Your Kitchen Experience...28

Welcome to a world where innovation meets flavor, and every dish is an opportunity to delight your senses. "Culinary Adventures with Ninja Air Fryer" is not just a cookbook; it's an invitation to reimagine your kitchen and embrace a new era of culinary delight. Let the journey begin!Chapter 1: Kitchen Mastery Basics.. 29

    Understanding Your Ninja Air Fryer........................ 30
    Essential Tools and Ingredients.............................31
    Tips for Efficient and Safe Cooking........................31

Chapter 2: 30-Day Starter Challenge........................ 33
    Week 1: Quick and Easy Air Fryer Essentials........ 33
    Week 2: Baking Bliss – Sweet and Savory.............34
    Week 3: Grilling Greatness with Your Ninja............ 34
    Week 4: Beyond Frying – Boiling and Roasting Tricks... 35

Chapter 3: Flavorful Adventures: Recipes Galore.. 37
    Section 1: Breakfast Bonanza............................... 39
    Section 2: Lunchtime Wonders.............................46
    Section 3: Dinner Delights..................................... 60
    Section 4: Snack Attack..74
    Section 5: Decadent Desserts............................... 81
        Triple Chocolate Fudge Brownie Delight Description: Indulge in the ultimate chocolate

experience with these fudgy brownies topped with three types of chocolate. Perfect for chocoholics!...81
Serving Size: 12 brownies....................81
Prep Time: 15 minutes.........................81
Cooking Time: 30 minutes....................81
Ingredients:...81
1 cup unsalted butter...........................82
2 cups sugar..82
4 big eggs..82
1 teaspoon vanilla extract....................82
1 cup all-purpose flour........................82
1/2 cup cocoa powder..........................82
1/4 teaspoon salt..................................82
1 cup semi-sweet chocolate chips......82
1 cup white chocolate chips................82
1 cup dark chocolate chunks..............82
Instructions:.. 82
Preheat oven to 350°F (175°C) and butter a 9x13 inch baking pan...........................82
In a large mixing basin, blend butter and sugar. Add eggs one at a time, beating thoroughly after each addition. Stir in vanilla.............................82
In a separate basin, whisk together flour, cocoa powder, and salt. Gradually add this dry mixture to the liquid components, mixing until just mixed.. 83
Fold in semi-sweet, white, and dark chocolate until uniformly distributed....................83
Pour the batter into the prepared pan and spread

it evenly..83

Bake for 30 minutes or until a toothpick inserted into the center comes out with moist crumbs, not wet batter.. 83

Allow to cool before cutting into sumptuous squares..83

2. Salted Caramel Cheesecake Heaven...........83

Description: A velvety cheesecake blended with ribbons of salted caramel, this dessert is a heavenly balance of sweetness and salty undertones..83

Serving Size: 10 slices.....................................83

Prep Time: 25 minutes.....................................83

Cooking Time: 1 hour and 15 minutes..............83

Ingredients:...83

2 cups graham cracker crumbs....................... 83

1/2 cup melted butter....................................... 84

4 packages (32 ounces) of cream cheese, softened.. 84

1 cup sugar.. 84

1 teaspoon vanilla extract................................ 84

4 big eggs.. 84

1 cup salted caramel sauce............................. 84

Instructions:... 84

Preheat the oven to 325°F (160°C) and butter a 9-inch springform pan.. 84

In a bowl, combine graham cracker crumbs and melted butter. Press the mixture into the bottom of the prepared pan to form the crust............... 84

In a large mixing basin, whisk cream cheese, sugar, and vanilla until creamy...........................84

Add eggs one at a time, mixing thoroughly after each addition..84

Pour half of the cheesecake batter over the crust. Drizzle half of the salted caramel sauce over the batter. Repeat with the remaining batter and caramel, creating a swirl appearance........85

Bake for 1 hour and 15 minutes or until the middle is firm...85

Allow the cheesecake to cool in the oven with the door ajar, then refrigerate for at least 4 hours before serving..85

3. Hazelnut Chocolate Mousse Parfait Description: Elevate your dessert experience with this exquisite hazelnut chocolate mousse parfait. Layers of creamy mousse and crunchy hazelnut praline create a wonderful symphony of textures..85

Serving Size: 6 parfaits....................................85

Prep Time: 30 minutes.....................................85

Cooking Time: 10 minutes................................85

Ingredients:...85

1 cup hazelnuts, roasted and chopped.............85

1 cup heavy cream...85

8 ounces bittersweet chocolate, chopped.........85

3 big eggs, separated......................................86

1/4 cup sugar...86

1 teaspoon vanilla extract................................86

Pinch of salt..86

Instructions:..86

In a saucepan, heat the heavy cream until just simmering. Remove from heat and add chopped chocolate. Stir until smooth. Let it cool to room temperature.. 86

In a bowl, whisk egg yolks with sugar until pale and creamy. Add vanilla essence and the cooled chocolate mixture. Mix until well blended......... 86

In a separate dish, beat egg whites with a pinch of salt until firm peaks form................................ 86

Gently incorporate the whipped egg whites into the chocolate mixture until no white streaks remain... 86

Layer the chocolate mousse with chopped hazelnuts in serving glasses or bowls.............. 86

Refrigerate for at least 4 hours or until the mousse is firm.. 86

Before serving, sprinkle the top with extra hazelnuts for added crunch.............................. 87

4. Raspberry White Chocolate Tart Extravaganza 87

Description: Delicate almond crust, delicious white chocolate ganache, and fresh raspberries come together in this visually gorgeous and tasty dessert... 87

Serving Size: 8 slices.. 87

Prep Time: 20 minutes....................................... 87

Cooking Time: 25 minutes.................................. 87

Ingredients: 1 1/2 cups almond flour.................. 87

1/4 cup melted butter... 87

1/3 cup powdered sugar.................................... 87

8 ounces white chocolate, chopped.................. 87

1/2 cup thick cream.. 87

1 teaspoon vanilla extract.................................. 87

2 cups fresh raspberries............................... 87
Instructions:.. 87
Preheat the oven to 350°F (175°C) and oil a tart pan.. 88
In a bowl, combine almond flour, melted butter, and powdered sugar. Press the mixture into the bottom and up the sides of the tart pan to form the crust.. 88
Bake the crust for 12-15 minutes or until lightly golden. Let it cool fully.. 88
In a heatproof bowl, add chopped white chocolate, heavy cream, and vanilla essence. Melt the chocolate over a double boiler or in the microwave in short bursts, stirring until smooth.... 88
Pour the white chocolate ganache into the cooled tart shell... 88
Arrange fresh raspberries on top of the ganache. 88
Refrigerate for at least 2 hours before serving. 88
5. Pistachio Rosewater Semolina Cake Description: Immerse yourself in the exotic tastes of this Middle Eastern-inspired cake. The mix of pistachios and rosewater creates a fragrant and nutty treat... 88
Serving Size: 10 slices...................................... 88
Prep Time: 25 minutes...................................... 89
Cooking Time: 45 minutes................................ 89
Ingredients:... 89
1 cup semolina... 89
1 cup pistachios, finely ground........................ 89

1 cup sugar..89
1 cup plain yogurt... 89
1/2 cup unsalted butter, melted..........................89
1/4 cup rosewater... 89
1 teaspoon baking powder.................................89
1/2 teaspoon baking soda..................................89
Pinch of salt.. 89
Instructions:... 89
Preheat the oven to 350°F (175°C) and butter a cake pan... 89
In a large bowl, combine semolina, ground pistachios, sugar, baking powder, baking soda, and salt... 89
In a separate bowl, stir together yogurt, melted butter, and rosewater... 90
Gradually add the wet components to the dry ingredients, mixing until just incorporated.........90
Pour the batter into the prepared cake pan and smooth the top... 90
Bake for 40-45 minutes or until a toothpick inserted into the center comes out clean.......... 90
Allow the cake to cool before slicing.................90
6. Mango Coconut Panna Cotta Bliss...............90
Description: Transport yourself to a tropical paradise with this velvety mango coconut panna cotta. A delicious and attractive dessert that's surprisingly easy to make.................................. 90
Serving Size: 6 servings.................................... 90
Prep Time: 20 minutes.......................................90
Setting Time: 4 hours (refrigeration) Ingredients:.

90

1 cup mango puree..90

1 cup coconut milk..90

1/2 cup sugar..91

2 teaspoons gelatin...91

2 tablespoons water..91

Fresh mango slices for garnish...........................91

Instructions:... 91

In a small bowl, sprinkle gelatin over water and let it bloom for 5 minutes....................................91

In a saucepan, boil mango puree, coconut milk, and sugar until it just begins to simmer. Remove from heat..91

Add the bloomed gelatin to the warm mango-coconut liquid, stirring until entirely dissolved..91

Strain the mixture to ensure a smooth texture..91

Pour the panna cotta mixture into serving glasses or molds..91

Refrigerate for at least 4 hours or until set........91

Garnish with fresh mango slices before serving... 91

7. Lemon Blueberry Mascarpone Tart...............91

Description: A balanced blend of acidic lemon, sweet blueberries, and creamy mascarpone, this tart is a burst of summer sensations in every bite. 92

Serving Size: 8 slices..92

Prep Time: 30 minutes.......................................92

Cooking Time: 25 minutes................................. 92

Ingredients: 92
1 1/2 cups all-purpose flour 92
1/2 cup powdered sugar 92
1/2 cup unsalted butter, cold and cubed 92
8 ounces mascarpone cheese 92
1/2 cup sugar Zest and juice of 2 lemons 92
2 big eggs 92
1 cup fresh blueberries 92
Instructions: 92
Preheat the oven to 375°F (190°C) and grease a tart pan 92
In a food processor, combine flour, powdered sugar, and cold cubed butter. Pulse until the mixture resembles coarse crumbs 93
Press the crust mixture into the tart pan, covering the bottom and up the sides. Chill for 15 minutes. 93
In a bowl, mix mascarpone, sugar, lemon zest, and lemon juice until creamy. Add eggs one at a time, mixing well 93
Pour the mascarpone filling into the cold crust. 93
Sprinkle fresh blueberries over the filling 93
Bake for 25 minutes or until the filling is set and the crust is brown 93
Allow the tart to cool before slicing 93
8. Caramel Pecan Chocolate Chip Cookie Bars ... 93
Description: Experience the ultimate cookie bar delight with layers of gooey caramel, crunchy nuts, and rich chocolate chips. A lovely take on regular chocolate chip cookies 93

Serving Size: 16 bars..93
Prep Time: 20 minutes..93
Cooking Time: 25 minutes..94
Ingredients:..94
2 1/4 cups all-purpose flour......................................94
1/2 teaspoon baking soda..94
1 cup unsalted butter, softened...............................94
1/2 cup granulated sugar..94
1 cup brown sugar, packed......................................94
2 big eggs..94
2 teaspoons vanilla extract.......................................94
1 cup chocolate chips..94
1 cup chopped pecans..94
1 cup caramel sauce..94
Instructions: Preheat the oven to 350°F (175°C) and line a baking pan with parchment paper....94
In a bowl, stir together flour and baking soda. Set aside..94
In a large mixing basin, beat together melted butter, granulated sugar, and brown sugar until light and fluffy...94
Add eggs one at a time, beating thoroughly after each addition. Stir in vanilla extract..................95
Gradually add the flour mixture to the wet ingredients, mixing until just mixed...................95
Fold in chocolate chips and chopped pecans...95
Press half of the cookie batter into the prepared pan. Pour caramel sauce over the dough.........95
Drop spoonfuls of the leftover cookie dough on top of the caramel...95

Bake for 25 minutes or until the edges are golden brown.. 95

Allow to cool before cutting into bars................ 95

9. Dark Chocolate Raspberry Truffle Cake Description: A sophisticated and delicious dark chocolate cake covered with velvety raspberry truffle filling. This dessert is a celebration of the timeless marriage of chocolate and raspberries... 95

Serving Size: 12 slices..95

Prep Time: 30 minutes..95

Cooking Time: 35 minutes................................. 96

Ingredients:... 96

1 3/4 cups all-purpose flour............................... 96

1 1/2 tablespoons baking powder...................... 96

1/2 teaspoon baking soda..................................96

1/2 cup unsweetened cocoa powder................ 96

1 1/2 cups granulated sugar.............................. 96

1/2 cup unsalted butter, softened......................96

2 big eggs... 96

1 teaspoon vanilla extract.................................. 96

1 cup buttermilk.. 96

8 ounces dark chocolate, chopped................... 96

1/2 cup thick cream..96

1 cup fresh raspberries...................................... 96

Instructions:... 96

Preheat the oven to 350°F (175°C) and butter and flour two 9-inch cake pans.......................... 96

In a bowl, whisk together flour, baking powder, baking soda, and cocoa powder. Set aside...... 97

In a large mixing basin, beat together sugar and melted butter until light and fluffy...................... 97

Add eggs one at a time, beating thoroughly after each addition. Stir in vanilla extract.................. 97

Gradually add the dry components to the wet ingredients, alternating with buttermilk, beginning and finishing with the dry ingredients. Mix until just mixed..97

Divide the batter between the prepared pans and smooth the tops... 97

Bake for 30-35 minutes or until a toothpick inserted into the center comes out clean.......... 97

While the cakes cool, make the raspberry truffle filling by melting dark chocolate with heavy cream. Allow it to cool.. 97

Once the cakes are cool, place a layer of raspberry truffle filling on top of one cake layer. Place the second layer on top and ice the entire cake with the remaining filling............................ 97

Garnish with fresh raspberries.......................... 98

10. Vanilla Bean Bourbon Creme Brulee.......... 98

Description: Elevate the classic crème brulee with the warm aromas of vanilla bean and a dash of bourbon. This exquisite dessert is excellent for special occasions...98

Serving Size: 6 servings................................... 98

Prep Time: 20 minutes......................................98

Cooking Time: 45 minutes................................ 98

Chilling Time: 4 hours....................................... 98

Ingredients:... 98

2 cups heavy cream..98

1 vanilla bean, split, and seeds scraped...........98

1/2 cup granulated sugar.................................98

4 big egg yolks..98

2 tablespoons bourbon....................................98

Brown sugar for caramelizing..........................98

Instructions:..98

Preheat the oven to 325°F (160°C) and set 6 ramekins in a baking dish............................... 99

In a saucepan, heat heavy cream and vanilla bean (seeds and pod) until it just begins to simmer. Remove from heat and let it soak for 15 minutes.. 99

In a bowl, mix sugar and egg yolks until pale... 99

Gradually add the cream mixture to the egg mixture, whisking constantly.............................. 99

Strain the custard to remove the vanilla bean pod...99

Stir in bourbon... 99

Divide the custard among the ramekins........... 99

Place the baking dish in the oven and pour hot water into the dish until it comes halfway up the edges of the ramekins....................................... 99

Bake for 40-45 minutes or until the custard is firm but still a little jiggly in the center...................... 99

Chill the crème brulee in the refrigerator for at least 4 hours before dusting a thin coating of brown sugar on top and caramelizing with a kitchen torch... 99

Section 6: Appetizers...100

Title: Caprese Skewers Description: A delicious spin on the traditional Caprese salad............. 100

Section 7: soups and salads..................................105
   1. Chicken Noodle Soup Description: Classic comfort food with a twist................................. 105
   Serving Size: 4...105
   Prep Time: 15 minutes....................................105
   Ingredients: 2 cups shredded cooked chicken 8 cups chicken broth...105
   1 cup chopped carrots..................................... 106
   1 cup diced celery..106
   1 cup egg noodles... 106
   1 teaspoon dried thyme.................................. 106
   Instructions: In a large saucepan, bring chicken stock to a boil... 106
   Add carrots, celery, and thyme. Simmer until veggies are soft... 106
   Stir in shredded chicken and egg noodles. Cook until the noodles are done............................. 106
   Season with salt and pepper to taste..............106
   2. Caprese Salad Description: A delicious Italian salad emphasizing tomatoes and mozzarella. 106
   Serving Size: 2 Prep Time: 10 minutes...........106
   Ingredients: 2 big tomatoes, sliced 1 cup fresh mozzarella, sliced 1/4 cup fresh basil leaves..107
   2 tablespoons balsamic glaze.........................107
   Salt and pepper to taste..................................107
   Instructions: Arrange tomato and mozzarella slices on a dish.. 107
   Tuck fresh basil leaves between slices............107
   Drizzle with balsamic glaze and season with salt and pepper...107

3. Minestrone Soup Description: Hearty Italian vegetable soup.. 107

Serving Size: 6..107

Prep Time: 20 minutes.....................................107

Ingredients: 1 cup diced onion.........................107

1 cup chopped carrots..................................... 108

1 cup diced zucchini.. 108

1 cup diced potatoes..108

1 can (15 oz) chopped tomatoes..................... 108

4 cups veggie broth 1 cup spaghetti shells.....108

Instructions: Sauté onions until transparent, add carrots, zucchini, and potatoes....................... 108

Stir in chopped tomatoes and veggie broth. Simmer until veggies are soft.......................... 108

Cook pasta separately and add to the soup before serving.. 108

4. Greek Salad Description: A bright and lively salad with Mediterranean tastes..................... 108

Serving Size: 4 Prep Time: 15 minutes...........108

Ingredients: 2 cups cherry tomatoes, halved 1 cucumber, diced 1 cup Kalamata olives, pitted 1 cup feta cheese, crumbled...............................109

1/4 cup red onion, thinly sliced........................ 109

2 tablespoons olive oil..................................... 109

1 tablespoon red wine vinegar........................ 109

Instructions:... 109

Combine tomatoes, cucumber, olives, feta, and red onion in a bowl...109

In a small bowl, mix olive oil and red wine vinegar... 109

Drizzle dressing over the salad and stir gently..... 109

5. Butternut Squash Soup Description: Creamy and flavorful fall-inspired soup........................ 109

Serving Size: 4...109

Prep Time: 25 minutes....................................109

Ingredients: 1 medium butternut squash, peeled and cubed 1 onion, chopped 2 cloves garlic, minced... 110

4 cups vegetable broth....................................110

1 teaspoon dried sage..................................... 110

Salt and pepper to taste.................................. 110

Instructions: Sauté onion and garlic until softened... 110

Add butternut squash, sage, and vegetable broth. Simmer until the squash is soft............. 110

Blend until smooth. Season with salt and pepper. 110

6. Caesar Salad Description: Classic Caesar salad with homemade dressing...................... 110

Serving Size: 2 Prep Time: 15 minutes........... 110

Ingredients: 1 head romaine lettuce, chopped 1/2 cup croutons.. 111

1/4 cup grated Parmesan cheese................... 111

1/4 cup Caesar dressing................................. 111

Instructions: Toss chopped lettuce with croutons and Parmesan...111

Drizzle Caesar dressing over the salad and toss until covered.. 111

7. Tomato Basil Soup Description: Rich and savory tomato soup with a dash of basil......... 111

Serving Size: 4 111
Prep Time: 20 minutes 111
Ingredients: 6 cups ripe tomatoes, chopped 1 onion, sliced 111
3 cloves garlic, minced 111
4 cups vegetable broth 111
1/2 cup fresh basil, chopped 112
Salt and pepper to taste 112
Instructions: Sauté onion and garlic until aromatic 112
Add tomatoes, vegetable broth, and basil. Simmer until tomatoes are tender 112
Blend until smooth. Season with salt and pepper. 112
8. Cobb Salad Description: A substantial salad with a blend of tastes and textures 112
Serving Size: 2 Prep Time: 15 minutes 112
Ingredients: 2 cups mixed greens 112
1 cup cooked chicken, diced 1 avocado, sliced 1/2 cup cherry tomatoes, halved 1/4 cup blue cheese, crumbled 2 hard-boiled eggs, sliced 1/4 cup ranch dressing 112
Instructions: Arrange mixed greens on a platter ... 112
Top with chicken, avocado, tomatoes, blue cheese, and eggs 113
Drizzle with ranch dressing 113
9. Mushroom Barley Soup Description: Hearty soup with earthy mushrooms and healthy barley .. 113
Serving Size: 6 Prep Time: 30 minutes 113

Ingredients: 1 cup pearl barley 113
1 cup diced onion 113
2 cups sliced mushrooms 113
4 cups vegetable broth 2 carrots, diced 113
2 celery stalks, chopped 113
directions: Cook barley according to package directions 113
Sauté onions and mushrooms until tender 114
Add barley, vegetable broth, carrots, and celery. Simmer until veggies are soft 114
10. Spinach Strawberry Salad Description: Light and refreshing salad with a fruity touch 114
Serving Size: 4 114
Prep Time: 15 minutes Ingredients: 114
4 cups baby spinach 114
1 cup sliced strawberries 114
1/2 cup candied pecans 114
1/4 cup feta cheese, crumbled 114
Balsamic vinaigrette dressing 114
Instructions: 114
Combine spinach, ... 115
Section 8: Side dishes 115
1. Garlic Parmesan Roasted Brussels Sprouts Description: A savory take on Brussels sprouts with crispy skin and a blast of garlic and Parmesan flavor 115
Serving Size: 4 115
Prep Time: 10 minutes 115
Ingredients: 1 lb Brussels sprouts, halved 115

2 tbsp olive oil..115
3 cloves garlic, minced....................................115
1/4 cup grated Parmesan cheese...................115
Salt and pepper to taste..................................115
Instructions:..115
Preheat oven to 400°F (200°C).......................115
Toss Brussels sprouts with olive oil, garlic, Parmesan, salt, and pepper............................115
Spread on a baking sheet and roast for 20-25 minutes until golden brown............................116
2. Mashed Sweet Potatoes with Cinnamon Butter Description: Creamy sweet potatoes mashed to perfection, topped with a fragrant cinnamon-infused butter.................................116
Serving Size: 6..116
Prep Time: 15 minutes....................................116
Ingredients: 4 huge sweet potatoes, peeled and cubed..116
1/2 cup unsalted butter...................................116
1 tsp ground cinnamon...................................116
Salt to taste..116
Instructions: Boil sweet potatoes until soft, then drain..116
Mash sweet potatoes and blend with butter, cinnamon, and salt until smooth.....................116
3. Quinoa and Vegetable Stir-Fry...................116
Description: A healthful side dish containing quinoa, bright veggies, and a soy-ginger sauce...116
Serving Size: 4 Prep Time: 20 minutes...........116

Ingredients: 1 cup quinoa, cooked................... 116
2 cups mixed veggies (bell peppers, broccoli, carrots).. 116
3 tbsp soy sauce... 116
1 tbsp sesame oil.. 116
1 tbsp fresh ginger, minced............................ 117
Instructions:... 117
Sauté veggies in sesame oil until crisp-tender...... 117
Add cooked quinoa, soy sauce, and ginger. Stir thoroughly and simmer for a further 3-4 minutes.. 117
4. Balsamic Glazed Roasted Asparagus Description: Roasted asparagus spears covered with a sweet and tart balsamic sauce............. 117
Serving Size: 4.. 117
Prep Time: 10 minutes..................................... 117
Ingredients: 1 pound asparagus, trimmed....... 117
2 tbsp olive oil... 117
3 tbsp balsamic vinegar.................................. 117
Salt and pepper to taste.................................. 117
Instructions: Toss asparagus with olive oil, balsamic vinegar, salt, and pepper.................. 117
Roast in a preheated oven at 425°F (220°C) for 15-20 minutes... 117
5. Lemon Herb Quinoa Salad Description: A delicious quinoa salad with a zesty lemon dressing and a variety of fresh herbs............... 117
Serving Size: 6.. 117
Prep Time: 15 minutes..................................... 118

Ingredients: 2 cups cooked quinoa................. 118

1/4 cup fresh parsley, chopped 2 tbsp fresh mint, chopped Zest and juice of 1 lemon................. 118

3 tbsp olive oil.. 118

Instructions: In a bowl, add quinoa, parsley, mint, lemon zest, lemon juice, and olive oil. Mix thoroughly..118

6. Creamy Garlic Parmesan Polenta Description: Silky and creamy polenta laced with garlic and Parmesan, a delightful side dish...................... 118

Serving Size: 4 Prep Time: 20 minutes........... 118

Ingredients:... 118

1 cup cornmeal... 118

4 cups chicken or veggie broth....................... 118

1/2 cup grated Parmesan cheese................... 118

3 cloves garlic, minced....................................118

Instructions:..118

Bring broth to a boil, gradually whisk in cornmeal, stirring continually...118

Stir in Parmesan and garlic, simmering until creamy..118

7. Honey-drizzled Carrots with Dill Description: Tender carrots drizzled in honey and garnished with fresh dill for a sweet and herbaceous taste... 119

Serving Size: 4.. 119

Prep Time: 15 minutes.................................... 119

Ingredients: 1 pound carrots, peeled and sliced... 119

2 tbsp honey... 119

2 tbsp butter.. 119
1 tbsp fresh dill, chopped............................... 119
Instructions:... 119
Boil or simmer carrots until soft....................... 119
In a pan, melt butter and honey. Add carrots and stir until covered. Sprinkle with dill................. 119
8. Caprese Salad Skewers Description: A bite-sized delicacy containing cherry tomatoes, mozzarella, and basil topped with balsamic sauce.. 119
Serving Size: 8 skewers.................................119
Prep Time: 15 minutes.................................. 119
Ingredients: 1-pint cherry tomatoes................ 119
8 ounce fresh mozzarella balls....................... 119
Fresh basil leaves.. 119
Balsamic glaze for drizzling............................ 119
Instructions: Thread a tomato, mozzarella ball, and basil leaf onto each skewer......................120
Arrange skewers on a plate and sprinkle with balsamic glaze... 120
9. Crispy Parmesan Zucchini Fries Description: Zucchini sticks covered with Parmesan and breadcrumbs, fried till golden and served with marinara sauce.. 120
Serving Size: 4...120
Prep Time: 20 minutes...................................120
Ingredients: 2 big zucchinis, sliced into fry..... 120
1 cup breadcrumbs.. 120
1/2 cup grated Parmesan............................... 120
2 eggs, beaten.. 120

Instructions:... 120

Dip zucchini sticks in beaten eggs, then cover in a combination of breadcrumbs and Parmesan..... 120

Bake in a preheated oven at 425°F (220°C) for 15-20 minutes... 120

10. Roasted Garlic and Rosemary Potatoes.. 120

Description: Crispy roasted potatoes blended with the tastes of garlic and rosemary............ 120

Serving Size: 6... 120

Prep Time: 15 minutes.................................. 120

Ingredients:.. 120

2 pounds young potatoes, halved 3 tbsp olive oil. 121

4 cloves garlic, minced 2 tbsp fresh rosemary, chopped... 121

Instructions:.. 121

Toss potatoes with olive oil, garlic, and rosemary. 121

Roast in a preheated oven at 400°F (200....... 121

Chapter 4: Mastering Ninja Air Fryer Techniques. 122

High level Air Searing Tips and Deceives............. 123

Idealizing Your Baking Abilities............................. 123

Barbecuing and Simmering Like a Master............ 124

Drying out for Solid Eating.................................... 124

Chapter 5: Affordable Culinary Magic.................... 125

Spending plan Cordial Fixing Replacements........ 126

Cash Saving Feast Arranging Procedures........... 127

Frugal Ninja Air Fryer Hacks................................. 127

Chapter 6: Culinary Wellness................................ 128

Dietary Advantages of Air Searing........................130
Good dieting Propensities with Your Ninja Air Fryer... 131
Careful Cooking for a Fair Way of Life..................132
Common Air Fryer Mistakes and Solutions.......... 135
 1. Uneven Cooking:................................... 135
 2. Food sticking to the basket:................... 136
 3. Rubbery Texture:...................................136
 4. Smoke Production:................................136
FAQs – Addressing Your Culinary Concerns........ 137
 Q1: Can I use parchment paper in my air fryer?..137
 Q2: Why is my food not getting crispy?.... 137
 Q3: How do I clean my air fryer?.............. 137

Chapter 8: Community Delights.............................139
Sharing Your Culinary Manifestations...................139
Online Assets and Networks................................141

Bonus Section: 30-Day Meal Plan..........................142
List and Index.. 164
Conclusion... 168

INTRODUCTION

Welcome to "Culinary Adventures with Ninja Air Fryer," where we embark on a journey to redefine your kitchen experience and elevate your culinary prowess. In this culinary haven, we unveil the artistry of the Ninja Air Fryer, a cutting-edge appliance designed to revolutionize the way you approach cooking.

Brief Overview of the Ninja Air Fryer

The Ninja Air Fryer is not just a kitchen gadget; it's a culinary companion that combines the precision of convection cooking with the efficiency of rapid air circulation. This powerhouse appliance lets you savor the flavors of your favorite dishes without compromising on health. From crispy golden fries to succulent meats, the Ninja Air Fryer promises to deliver delectable results with a fraction of the oil traditionally used.

How This Cookbook Will Transform Your Kitchen Experience

Our cookbook is not merely a collection of recipes; it's a roadmap to culinary excellence. We have curated a diverse repertoire of dishes that showcase the versatility of the Ninja Air Fryer, ensuring that every meal becomes a masterpiece. Whether you're a seasoned chef or a kitchen novice, our step-by-step instructions and expert tips will empower you to unleash your inner culinary artist.

Prepare to embark on a culinary adventure where the Ninja Air Fryer becomes your trusted ally, transforming mundane meals into extraordinary experiences. Get ready to savor the thrill of culinary exploration as we guide you through a tantalizing array of recipes, each crafted to elevate your kitchen endeavors.

Welcome to a world where innovation meets flavor, and every dish is an opportunity to delight your senses. "Culinary Adventures with Ninja Air Fryer" is not just a cookbook; it's an invitation to reimagine your kitchen and embrace a new era of culinary delight. Let the journey begin!

Chapter 1: Kitchen Mastery Basics

Embark on a culinary journey as we delve into the fundamentals of kitchen mastery in this comprehensive guide to Chapter 1. Discover the intricacies of understanding your Ninja Air Fryer, unlocking its full potential to elevate your cooking experience.

Understanding Your Ninja Air Fryer

Unlock the secrets of your culinary ally, the Ninja Air Fryer. Dive into a detailed exploration of its features, functions, and how to harness its power for optimal results. From mastering temperature control to unleashing the full spectrum of cooking modes, this section provides a roadmap to elevate your kitchen expertise.

Essential Tools and Ingredients

Equip yourself with the indispensable tools and premium ingredients that form the backbone of kitchen mastery. Explore a curated list of must-have kitchen gadgets and utensils, ensuring you're armed with everything needed to execute recipes flawlessly. Uncover the importance of quality ingredients, elevating your dishes from ordinary to extraordinary.

Tips for Efficient and Safe Cooking

Safety meets efficiency in this crucial section. Uncover practical tips and techniques that not only enhance your cooking efficiency but also prioritize safety in the kitchen. From proper handling of kitchen tools to understanding crucial safety protocols, empower yourself with the knowledge to create culinary masterpieces without compromising on well-being.

Engage with this chapter as it unveils the cornerstone principles of kitchen mastery, providing a solid foundation for your culinary aspirations. Whether you're a novice or a seasoned chef, these insights will guide you toward becoming a maestro in your kitchen, transforming every cooking endeavor into a delightful and rewarding experience.

Chapter 2: 30-Day Starter Challenge

Embark on a culinary journey with our 30-Day Starter Challenge, where each week unveils a new realm of gastronomic delight.

Week 1: Quick and Easy Air Fryer Essentials

Dive into the world of efficient cooking with the air fryer. From crispy fries to succulent chicken wings, this week will transform your kitchen routine. Discover time-saving hacks and flavorful shortcuts that make every meal a breeze.

Week 2: Baking Bliss – Sweet and Savory

Indulge your sweet tooth and explore the savory side of baking. Week 2 is a celebration of dough, batter, and the heavenly aroma of freshly baked creations. Elevate your baking skills with delectable pastries, bread, and mouthwatering desserts that redefine the art of homemade goodness.

Week 3: Grilling Greatness with Your Ninja

Fire up the Ninja and embrace the sizzle! Week 3 invites you to master the art of grilling. From perfectly seared steaks to vibrant grilled veggies, unlock the secrets to achieving that coveted smoky flavor. Elevate your outdoor cooking game and become a grilling maestro.

Week 4: Beyond Frying – Boiling and Roasting Tricks

In the final week, we push culinary boundaries. Move beyond the familiar as we explore boiling and roasting techniques that add depth and richness to your dishes. Uncover the nuances of simmering perfection and the magic of roasting, ensuring your meals reach new heights of flavor.

Join us on this 30-Day Starter Challenge, where each week unfolds a culinary adventure. Elevate your cooking skills, tantalize your taste buds, and make each meal a masterpiece. Are you ready to transform your kitchen into a realm of culinary excellence?

Chapter 3: Flavorful Adventures: Recipes Galore

Embark on a culinary journey with "Flavorful Adventures: Recipes Galore," a chapter that tantalizes the taste buds and elevates your culinary prowess. In this immersive exploration, we delve into a treasure trove of delectable recipes that promise to ignite your passion for the art of cooking. Unleash your inner chef as you navigate through a diverse array of mouthwatering dishes, each crafted to perfection. From exotic appetizers that set the stage for a memorable meal to sumptuous main courses that redefine your culinary expectations, this chapter is a celebration of flavors from around the world.

Discover the secrets behind signature dishes that have stood the test of time, as well as innovative creations that push the boundaries of traditional gastronomy. Whether you're a seasoned chef or a novice in the kitchen, "Flavorful Adventures" provides step-by-step guides and expert tips to ensure your culinary success.

The chapter not only focuses on the result but also immerses you in the stories behind each recipe. Gain insights into the cultural origins, historical significance, and personal anecdotes that make these dishes truly special. It's more than just cooking; it's an exploration of the rich tapestry of global cuisines.

As you turn the pages of "Flavorful Adventures," you'll find that the journey goes beyond the kitchen. It's a sensory experience that engages sight, smell, and taste, bringing the joy of cooking to life. Each recipe is a chapter in itself, telling a story of tradition, innovation, and the joy of sharing meals with loved ones.

Prepare to elevate your culinary skills, expand your flavor palate, and create lasting memories with "Flavorful Adventures: Recipes Galore." Whether you're seeking a quick weekday meal or planning an elaborate feast, this chapter is your passport to a world of delicious possibilities. Let the culinary odyssey begin!

Section 1: Breakfast Bonanza

Savory Veggie Omelette Description: A wonderful omelette loaded with colorful veggies.

Serving Size: 2 Prep Time: 10 minutes

Cooking Time: 10 minutes

Ingredients: Eggs, bell peppers, onions, tomatoes, cheese, salt, and pepper.

Instructions: Beat eggs, sauté vegetables, pour eggs over veggies, simmer until set.

Blueberry Banana Pancakes Description: Fluffy pancakes with the flavor of blueberries and bananas.

Serving Size: 4 Prep Time: 15 minutes

Cooking Time: 15 minutes

Ingredients: Pancake mix, blueberries, bananas, milk, vanilla essence.

Instructions: Mix ingredients, heat on the griddle, and turn when bubbles appear.

Greek Yogurt Parfait Description: Layers of Greek yogurt, granola, and fresh berries.

Serving Size: 1 Prep Time: 5 minutes

Cooking Time: 0 minutes

Ingredients: Greek yogurt, granola, strawberries, blueberries, honey.

Instructions: Layer ingredients in a glass, and drizzle with honey.

Avocado Toast with Poached Egg Description: Creamy avocado on toast topped with a flawlessly poached egg.

Serving Size: 2 Prep Time: 10 minutes

Cooking Time: 5 minutes

Ingredients: Bread, avocado, eggs, salt, pepper, chili flakes.

Instructions: Toast bread, spread avocado, poached egg, season.

Chocolate Banana Smoothie Bowl Description: A nutritious and tasty smoothie bowl for breakfast.

Serving Size: 1 Prep Time: 5 minutes

Cooking Time: 0 minutes

Ingredients: Frozen banana, chocolate powder, almond milk, toppings.

Instructions: Blend ingredients, pour into a bowl, add toppings.

Breakfast Burritos Description: Hearty burritos loaded with eggs, sausage, and vegetables.

Serving Size: 4 Prep Time: 15 minutes

Cooking Time: 10 minutes

Ingredients: Tortillas, eggs, sausage, bell peppers, onions, cheese.

Instructions: Cook ingredients, fill tortillas, wrap into burritos.

Classic French Toast Description: Thick slices of bread drowned in a sweet cinnamon egg concoction.

Serving Size: 3 Prep Time: 10 minutes

Cooking Time: 10 minutes

Ingredients: Bread, eggs, milk, cinnamon, vanilla essence.

Instructions: Dip bread in egg mixture, and fry till golden.

Quinoa Breakfast meal Description: Nutrient-packed quinoa meal with fruits and almonds.

Serving Size: 2 Prep Time: 15 minutes

Cooking Time: 15 minutes

Ingredients: Quinoa, almond milk, bananas, almonds, honey.

Instructions: Cook quinoa, top with fruits and nuts, sprinkle honey.

Spinach & Feta Egg Muffins Description: Portable egg muffins with spinach and feta cheese.

Serving Size: 6 Prep Time: 10 minutes

Cooking Time: 20 minutes

Ingredients: Eggs, spinach, feta cheese, salt, pepper.

Instructions: Mix ingredients, pour into muffin cups, bake.

Peanut Butter Banana Toast Description: A fast and tasty toast with peanut butter and banana.

Serving Size: 1 Prep Time: 5 minutes

Cooking Time: 0 minutes

Ingredients: Bread, peanut butter, banana slices, honey.

Instructions: Toast bread, spread peanut butter, top with banana, and pour honey.

Section 2: Lunchtime Wonders

Title: Classic Chicken Caesar Salad Description: A classic favorite with crisp romaine lettuce, grilled chicken, and a zesty Caesar dressing.

Serving Size: 4 Prep Time: 15 minutes

Cooking Time: 15 minutes

Ingredients: 2 boneless, skinless chicken breasts

1 head romaine lettuce

1 cup cherry tomatoes, halved

1/2 cup croutons

1/2 cup grated Parmesan cheese

Caesar dressing

Instructions:

Grill chicken breasts until thoroughly done, then slice into strips.

Wash and cut romaine lettuce, putting it in a big bowl.

Add sliced chicken, cherry tomatoes, croutons, and Parmesan cheese.

Drizzle Caesar dressing over the salad and stir gently.

2. Title: Veggie Pesto Pasta Description: A colorful and savory pasta meal incorporating fresh veggies and a tasty pesto sauce.

Serving Size: 6 Prep Time: 20 minutes

Cooking Time: 15 minutes

Ingredients: 12 oz pasta

1 cup cherry tomatoes, halved 1 zucchini, sliced 1 bell pepper, diced 1/2 cup black olives, sliced 1/2 cup pesto sauce

directions: Cook pasta according to package directions; drain and put aside.

In a skillet, sauté zucchini, bell pepper, and cherry tomatoes until soft.

Combine cooked pasta, sautéed veggies, black olives, and pesto sauce in a big bowl.

3. Title: Quinoa and Black Bean dish Description: A protein-packed dish with quinoa, black beans, avocado, and a zesty lime vinaigrette.

Serving Size: 3 Prep Time: 15 minutes

Cooking Time: 20 minutes

Ingredients:

1 cup quinoa

1 can black beans, drained and rinsed

1 avocado, diced

1 cup corn kernels

1/4 cup fresh cilantro, chopped

Lime dressing

directions: Cook quinoa according to package directions.

In a bowl, mix quinoa, black beans, avocado, corn, and cilantro.

Drizzle with lime dressing and mix gently.

4. Title: Caprese Sandwich

Description: A wonderful sandwich with fresh mozzarella, luscious tomatoes, basil, and a balsamic glaze.

Serving Size: 2 Prep Time: 10 minutes

Cooking Time: 5 minutes

Ingredients: 4 pieces of bread

1 big tomato, cut 8 oz fresh mozzarella, sliced

Fresh basil leaves

Balsamic glaze

Instructions:

Toast bread slices till golden brown.

Layer tomato slices, fresh mozzarella, and basil leaves between the toasted bread.

Drizzle with balsamic glaze and arrange into sandwiches.

5. Title: Spicy Chickpea Wraps Description: A spicy and delicious wrap containing seasoned chickpeas, crisp vegetables, and a creamy tahini sauce.

Serving Size: 4

Prep Time: 15 minutes

Cooking Time: 10 minutes

Ingredients: 2 cans chickpeas, drained and rinsed

1 tablespoon olive oil

1 teaspoon cumin

1 teaspoon paprika

1/2 teaspoon cayenne pepper

4 whole wheat wraps

Shredded lettuce, chopped tomatoes, sliced cucumber

Tahini sauce

Instructions:

In a skillet, sauté chickpeas with olive oil, cumin, paprika, and cayenne pepper until golden.

Assemble wraps with chickpeas, lettuce, tomatoes, and cucumber, and sprinkle with tahini sauce.

6. Title: Teriyaki fish dish Description: A tasty dish including teriyaki-glazed fish, brown rice, and a vibrant mix of veggies.

Serving Size: 2 Prep Time: 15 minutes

Cooking Time: 15 minutes

Ingredients: 2 salmon fillets

1 cup brown rice, cooked

1 cup broccoli florets

1 carrot, julienned

1/2 cup snap peas

Teriyaki sauce

Instructions:

Grill or pan-sear salmon fillets until cooked through.

Steam broccoli, carrots, and snap peas until tender-crisp.

Assemble bowls with cooked brown rice, veggies, and teriyaki-glazed fish.

7. Title: Mediterranean Quinoa Salad Description: A delightful salad with quinoa, cucumber, cherry tomatoes, olives, and feta cheese in a lemon vinaigrette.

Serving Size: 4 Prep Time: 20 minutes

Cooking Time: 15 minutes

Ingredients: 1 cup quinoa

1 cucumber, diced

1 cup cherry tomatoes, halved

1/2 cup Kalamata olives, sliced 1/2 cup feta cheese, crumbled

Lemon vinaigrette

directions: Cook quinoa according to package directions.

In a large bowl, mix quinoa, cucumber, cherry tomatoes, olives, and feta cheese.

Drizzle with lemon vinaigrette and stir gently.

8. Title: Turkey and Avocado Wrap Description: A protein-packed wrap with lean turkey, creamy avocado, lettuce, and a tangy yogurt dressing.

Serving Size: 2 Prep Time: 10 minutes

Cooking Time: 5 minutes

Ingredients: 8 oz turkey slices

1 avocado, sliced

Shredded lettuce

Whole wheat wraps

Greek yogurt dressing

Instructions: Warm turkey slices in a pan for a few minutes.

Assemble wraps with turkey, avocado, and lettuce, and sprinkle with Greek yogurt dressing.

9. Title: Lentil and Vegetable Soup Description: Hearty and healthy soup with lentils, carrots, celery, and spinach in a delicious broth.

Serving Size: 6 Prep Time: 15 minutes

Cooking Time: 30 minutes

Ingredients: 1 cup dry green lentils

2 carrots, chopped

2 celery stalks, chopped 1 onion, finely chopped

3 cups fresh spinach

Vegetable broth

Instructions: Rinse lentils and boil in vegetable broth until soft.

Sauté carrots, celery, and onion until softened.

Add sautéed veggies and spinach to the lentils, cooking until flavors blend.

10. Title: Shrimp and Avocado Salad Description: A light and delicious salad with juicy shrimp, creamy avocado, and a zesty lime dressing.

Serving Size: 4 Prep Time: 20 minutes

Cooking Time: 5 minutes

Ingredients: 1 pound shrimp, peeled and deveined

2 avocados, diced

Mixed salad greens

Cherry tomatoes, halved

Lime dressing

Instructions: Sauté shrimp in a skillet until pink and opaque.

In a large bowl, add shrimp, chopped avocados, salad leaves, and cherry tomatoes.

Drizzle with lime dressing and gently stir before serving.

Section 3: Dinner Delights

1. Grilled Lemon Herb Chicken Description: A refreshing and tasty meal suitable for summer nights.

Serving Size: 4 Prep Time: 15 minutes

Cooking Time: 20 minutes

Ingredients:

4 boneless, skinless chicken breasts

1/4 cup olive oil

3 tablespoons fresh lemon juice

2 cloves garlic, minced

1 teaspoon dried oregano

Salt and pepper to taste

Instructions:

In a bowl, combine olive oil, lemon juice, minced garlic, oregano, salt, and pepper.

Marinate chicken breasts in the mixture for 10 minutes.

Preheat grill and cook chicken for 8-10 minutes each side until well done.

2. Creamy Mushroom Risotto Description: A delicious and comforting Italian classic with a creamy touch.

Serving Size: 6

Prep Time: 10 minutes

Cooking Time: 25 minutes

Ingredients: 1 1/2 cups Arborio rice

1 cup sliced mushrooms

4 cups chicken or veggie broth

1/2 cup dry white wine

1/2 cup grated Parmesan cheese

1/4 cup heavy cream

Instructions: Sauté mushrooms in olive oil till golden brown.

Add Arborio rice and heat until gently toasted.

Pour in white wine and let it soak.

Gradually add broth, stirring until rice is creamy.

Stir in Parmesan and heavy cream before serving.

3. Spaghetti Bolognese

Description: A substantial and typical Italian beef sauce served over al dente pasta.

Serving Size: 4 Prep Time: 15 minutes

Cooking Time: 30 minutes

Ingredients:

1 pound ground beef

1 onion, finely chopped 2 cloves garlic, minced

1 can mashed tomatoes

1/2 cup red wine

1 teaspoon dried basil

Salt and pepper to taste

Instructions: Brown ground beef in a skillet, then add chopped onion and garlic.

Stir in smashed tomatoes, red wine, basil, salt, and pepper.

Simmer on low heat for 20 minutes.

Serve over cooked pasta.

4. Honey Soy Glazed Fish Description: A sweet and savory glaze turns fish into a delightful supper.

Serving Size: 2 Prep Time: 10 minutes

Cooking Time: 15 minutes

Ingredients: 2 salmon fillets

3 tablespoons soy sauce

2 tablespoons honey

1 tablespoon olive oil

1 teaspoon minced ginger

2 cloves garlic, minced

Instructions: Mix soy sauce, honey, olive oil, ginger, and garlic.

Brush the glaze over the salmon fillets.

Bake or pan-sear fish until cooked through.

5. Vegetarian Chickpea Curry Description: A delicious and protein-packed vegetarian curry.

Serving Size: 4

Prep Time: 15 minutes

Cooking Time: 25 minutes

Ingredients: 2 cans chickpeas, drained

1 onion, diced 2 tomatoes, chopped

1 cup coconut milk

2 teaspoons curry powder

1 teaspoon cumin

Salt and pepper to taste

Instructions: Sauté sliced onion till golden brown.

Add diced tomatoes, chickpeas, coconut milk, curry powder, cumin, salt, and pepper.

Simmer until flavors mingle.

6. Stuffed Bell Peppers Description: Colorful bell peppers packed with a delectable blend of rice, beans, and spices.

Serving Size: 6 Prep Time: 20 minutes

Cooking Time: 35 minutes

Ingredients:

6 bell peppers, halved

1 cup cooked rice

1 can black beans, drained

1 cup corn kernels

1 cup salsa

1 teaspoon cumin

Shredded cheese for topping

Instructions:

Preheat oven to 375°F (190°C).

Mix rice, black beans, corn, salsa, and cumin.

Stuff bell peppers with the mixture, cover with cheese and bake until peppers are soft.

7. Lemon Garlic Shrimp Pasta

Description: A zesty and fast pasta meal with delicious shrimp.

Serving Size: 2

Prep Time: 10 minutes

Cooking Time: 15 minutes

Ingredients: 8 oz linguine

1/2 pound shrimp, peeled and deveined

3 tablespoons olive oil

3 cloves garlic, minced Zest, and juice of 1 lemon

Red pepper flakes (optional)

directions: Cook linguine according to package directions.

Sauté shrimp and chopped garlic in olive oil until shrimp are pink.

Toss cooked pasta with shrimp, lemon zest, lemon juice, and red pepper flakes.

8. Teriyaki Chicken Stir-Fry

Description: A fast and tasty stir-fry with delicate chicken and crisp veggies.

Serving Size: 4

Prep Time: 15 minutes

Cooking Time: 20 minutes

Ingredients: 1 lb boneless, skinless chicken, thinly sliced

2 cups broccoli florets

1 bell pepper, sliced

1/2 cup teriyaki sauce

2 teaspoons soy sauce

1 tablespoon sesame oil

Instructions:

Stir-fry chicken until browned, then put aside.

Sauté broccoli and bell pepper in sesame oil.

Add cooked chicken back to the pan, pour in teriyaki sauce and soy sauce, and stir until well-coated.

9. Mushroom Spinach Quiche (Continued)

Description: A lovely quiche loaded with earthy mushrooms and colorful spinach.

Serving Size: 8 Prep Time: 20 minutes

Cooking Time: 40 minutes

Ingredients:

1 pre-made pie crust

1 cup sliced mushrooms

2 cups fresh spinach, chopped

1 cup shredded Gruyère cheese

4 big eggs

1 cup milk

Salt and pepper to taste

Instructions:

Preheat oven to 375°F (190°C).

In a skillet, sauté mushrooms until brown, then add spinach and simmer until wilted.

Line pie crust with the mushroom and spinach mixture, top with Gruyère.

In a bowl, mix eggs, milk, salt, and pepper. Pour over the veggies and cheese.

Bake until the quiche is set and golden brown on top.

10. BBQ Pulled Pork Tacos Description: Flavor-packed pulled pork tacos with a BBQ twist.

Serving Size: 6

Prep Time: 15 minutes

Cooking Time: 6 hours (slow cooker)

Ingredients: 2 pounds pork shoulder, trimmed

1 cup barbecue sauce

1 onion, sliced

2 cloves garlic, minced

1 tablespoon chili powder

1 teaspoon cumin

Corn tortillas

Toppings: shredded cabbage, cilantro, lime wedges

Instructions:

Rub pork shoulder with chili powder, cumin, and salt.

Place pork in a slow cooker, and cover with chopped onion, minced garlic, and barbecue sauce.

Cook on low for 6 hours or until meat is tender.

Shred pork and serve in corn tortillas with your favorite toppings.

Section 4: Snack Attack

Spicy Sriracha Popcorn Description: Elevate your snack game with this spicy spin on regular popcorn.

Serving Size: 4 cups

Prep Time: 5 minutes

Cooking Time: 5 minutes

Ingredients: 1/3 cup popcorn kernels

2 tbsp melted butter

1 tbsp Sriracha sauce

1/2 tsp smoked paprika

Salt to taste

Instructions:

Pop the popcorn kernels.

In a bowl, combine melted butter, Sriracha, smoked paprika, and salt.

Drizzle the spicy sauce over the popcorn, twisting to cover evenly.

2. Cheesy Avocado Bruschetta

Description: A delicious mix of creamy avocado and cheese bliss over crunchy toast.

Serving Size: 6 pieces

Prep Time: 10 minutes

Cooking Time: 5 minutes

Ingredients: 1 baguette, sliced 2 ripe avocados

1 cup shredded mozzarella

2 tbsp olive oil

Salt and pepper to taste

Instructions: Toast baguette slices until browned.

Mash avocados and put them over each slice.

Sprinkle mozzarella, drizzle with olive oil, and season with salt and pepper.

3. Pesto Tortilla Pizza Bites Description: Quick and tasty small pizzas with a spicy pesto twist.

Serving Size: 8 pieces

Prep Time: 8 minutes

Cooking Time: 7 minutes

Ingredients: 4 tiny wheat tortillas

1/2 cup pesto sauce

1 cup cherry tomatoes, halved

1 cup shredded Parmesan

Fresh basil leaves for garnish

Instructions:

Preheat oven to 400°F (200°C).

Spread pesto on tortillas, add tomatoes, then top with Parmesan.

Bake until the edges are golden. Garnish with fresh basil.

4. Honey Mustard Pretzel morsels Description: Sweet and tangy morsels that mix the crunch of pretzels with the richness of honey mustard.

Serving Size: 2 cups

Prep Time: 15 minutes

Cooking Time: 10 minutes

Ingredients:

2 cups pretzel bites

3 tbsp honey

2 tbsp Dijon mustard

1 tbsp melted butter

1/2 tsp garlic powder

Instructions:

Bake pretzel nibbles as per package directions.

In a bowl, combine honey, Dijon mustard, melted butter, and garlic powder.

Toss pretzel bits in the honey mustard sauce until covered.

5. Mango Salsa Nachos Description: A tropical spin on conventional nachos with vivid mango salsa.

Serving Size: 4 servings

Prep Time: 12 minutes

Cooking Time: 8 minutes

Ingredients: 1 package tortilla chips

1 cup diced mango

1/2 cup black beans, washed

1 cup shredded cheddar cheese

1/4 cup chopped cilantro

Instructions: Arrange tortilla chips on a baking pan.

Sprinkle with black beans, mango, and cheese.

Bake until the cheese melts. Top with cilantro.

6. Cucumber Hummus Cups Description: Refreshing cucumber cups packed with creamy hummus for a light and pleasant snack.

Serving Size: 12 cups

Prep Time: 15 minutes

Cooking Time: 0 minutes

Ingredients:

2 cucumbers, cut into rounds

1 cup hummus

Cherry tomatoes for garnish

Fresh dill for garnish

Instructions: Scoop out a tiny well in each cucumber round.

Fill each well with hummus.

Garnish with cherry tomatoes and fresh dill.

7. Buffalo Cauliflower Bites Description: Crispy and spicy buffalo-flavored cauliflower bites for a healthier spin on buffalo wings.

Serving Size: 4 servings

Prep Time: 15 minutes

Cooking Time: 25 minutes

Ingredients:

1 cauliflower head, sliced into florets

1/2 cup buffalo sauce

1/4 cup melted butter

1 tsp garlic powder

Instructions:

Preheat oven to 450°F (230°C).

Toss cauliflower with buffalo sauce, melted butter, and garlic powder.

Bake until crispy, approximately 25 minutes.

8. Greek Yogurt Berry Parfait Description: A nourishing and delightful parfait with layers of Greek yogurt, fresh berries, and granola.

Serving Size: 2 parfaits

Prep Time: 10 minutes

Cooking Time: 0 minutes

Ingredients: 1 cup Greek yogurt

1 cup mixed berries (strawberries, blueberries, raspberries)

1/2 cup granola

Honey for drizzling

Instructions: In serving glasses, layer Greek yogurt, berries, and granola.

Repeat layers and end with a sprinkle of honey.

9. Caprese Skewers with Balsamic Glaze Description: Elegant and tasty skewers with the traditional Caprese mix.

Serving Size: 12 skewers

Prep Time: 15 minutes

Cooking Time: 0 minutes

Ingredients:

24 cherry tomatoes

24 fresh mozzarella balls

Fresh basil leaves

Balsamic glaze for drizzling

Instructions: Thread a tomato, mozzarella ball, and basil leaf onto each skewer.

Arrange on a serving dish and drizzle with balsamic glaze.

10. Chocolate-Dipped Banana Bites Description: A delicious and pleasant delicacy with the traditional mix of chocolate and bananas.

Serving Size: 16 pieces

Prep Time: 20 minutes

Cooking Time: 5 minutes

Ingredients: 4 ripe bananas, sliced 1 cup dark chocolate chips, melted

Chopped nuts or coconut flakes (optional)

Instructions:

Dip banana slices into melted chocolate.

Place on a parchment-lined tray and sprinkle with nuts or coconut.

Allow to set in the refrigerator before serving.

Section 5: Decadent Desserts

Triple Chocolate Fudge Brownie Delight Description:

Indulge in the ultimate chocolate experience with these fudgy brownies topped with three types of chocolate. Perfect for chocoholics!

Serving Size: 12 brownies

Prep Time: 15 minutes

Cooking Time: 30 minutes

Ingredients:

1 cup unsalted butter

2 cups sugar

4 big eggs

1 teaspoon vanilla extract

1 cup all-purpose flour

1/2 cup cocoa powder

1/4 teaspoon salt

1 cup semi-sweet chocolate chips

1 cup white chocolate chips

1 cup dark chocolate chunks

Instructions:

Preheat oven to 350°F (175°C) and butter a 9x13 inch baking pan.

In a large mixing basin, blend butter and sugar. Add eggs one at a time, beating thoroughly after each addition. Stir in vanilla.

In a separate basin, whisk together flour, cocoa powder, and salt. Gradually add this dry mixture to the liquid components, mixing until just mixed.

Fold in semi-sweet, white, and dark chocolate until uniformly distributed.

Pour the batter into the prepared pan and spread it evenly.

Bake for 30 minutes or until a toothpick inserted into the center comes out with moist crumbs, not wet batter.

Allow to cool before cutting into sumptuous squares.

2. Salted Caramel Cheesecake Heaven

Description: A velvety cheesecake blended with ribbons of salted caramel, this dessert is a heavenly balance of sweetness and salty undertones.

Serving Size: 10 slices

Prep Time: 25 minutes

Cooking Time: 1 hour and 15 minutes

Ingredients:

2 cups graham cracker crumbs

1/2 cup melted butter

4 packages (32 ounces) of cream cheese, softened

1 cup sugar

1 teaspoon vanilla extract

4 big eggs

1 cup salted caramel sauce

Instructions:

Preheat the oven to 325°F (160°C) and butter a 9-inch springform pan.

In a bowl, combine graham cracker crumbs and melted butter. Press the mixture into the bottom of the prepared pan to form the crust.

In a large mixing basin, whisk cream cheese, sugar, and vanilla until creamy.

Add eggs one at a time, mixing thoroughly after each addition.

Pour half of the cheesecake batter over the crust. Drizzle half of the salted caramel sauce over the batter. Repeat with the remaining batter and caramel, creating a swirl appearance.

Bake for 1 hour and 15 minutes or until the middle is firm.

Allow the cheesecake to cool in the oven with the door ajar, then refrigerate for at least 4 hours before serving.

3. Hazelnut Chocolate Mousse Parfait Description: Elevate your dessert experience with this exquisite

hazelnut chocolate mousse parfait. Layers of creamy mousse and crunchy hazelnut praline create a wonderful symphony of textures.

Serving Size: 6 parfaits

Prep Time: 30 minutes

Cooking Time: 10 minutes

Ingredients:

1 cup hazelnuts, roasted and chopped

1 cup heavy cream

8 ounces bittersweet chocolate, chopped

3 big eggs, separated

1/4 cup sugar

1 teaspoon vanilla extract

Pinch of salt

Instructions:

In a saucepan, heat the heavy cream until just simmering. Remove from heat and add chopped chocolate. Stir until smooth. Let it cool to room temperature.

In a bowl, whisk egg yolks with sugar until pale and creamy. Add vanilla essence and the cooled chocolate mixture. Mix until well blended.

In a separate dish, beat egg whites with a pinch of salt until firm peaks form.

Gently incorporate the whipped egg whites into the chocolate mixture until no white streaks remain.

Layer the chocolate mousse with chopped hazelnuts in serving glasses or bowls.

Refrigerate for at least 4 hours or until the mousse is firm.

Before serving, sprinkle the top with extra hazelnuts for added crunch.

4. Raspberry White Chocolate Tart Extravaganza

Description: Delicate almond crust, delicious white chocolate ganache, and fresh raspberries come together in this visually gorgeous and tasty dessert.

Serving Size: 8 slices

Prep Time: 20 minutes

Cooking Time: 25 minutes

Ingredients: 1 1/2 cups almond flour

1/4 cup melted butter

1/3 cup powdered sugar

8 ounces white chocolate, chopped

1/2 cup thick cream

1 teaspoon vanilla extract

2 cups fresh raspberries

Instructions:

Preheat the oven to 350°F (175°C) and oil a tart pan.

In a bowl, combine almond flour, melted butter, and powdered sugar. Press the mixture into the bottom and up the sides of the tart pan to form the crust.

Bake the crust for 12-15 minutes or until lightly golden. Let it cool fully.

In a heatproof bowl, add chopped white chocolate, heavy cream, and vanilla essence. Melt the chocolate over a double boiler or in the microwave in short bursts, stirring until smooth.

Pour the white chocolate ganache into the cooled tart shell.

Arrange fresh raspberries on top of the ganache.

Refrigerate for at least 2 hours before serving.

5. Pistachio Rosewater Semolina Cake Description: Immerse yourself in the exotic tastes of this Middle Eastern-inspired cake. The mix of pistachios and rosewater creates a fragrant and nutty treat.

Serving Size: 10 slices

Prep Time: 25 minutes

Cooking Time: 45 minutes

Ingredients:

1 cup semolina

1 cup pistachios, finely ground

1 cup sugar

1 cup plain yogurt

1/2 cup unsalted butter, melted

1/4 cup rosewater

1 teaspoon baking powder

1/2 teaspoon baking soda

Pinch of salt

Instructions:

Preheat the oven to 350°F (175°C) and butter a cake pan.

In a large bowl, combine semolina, ground pistachios, sugar, baking powder, baking soda, and salt.

In a separate bowl, stir together yogurt, melted butter, and rosewater.

Gradually add the wet components to the dry ingredients, mixing until just incorporated.

Pour the batter into the prepared cake pan and smooth the top.

Bake for 40-45 minutes or until a toothpick inserted into the center comes out clean.

Allow the cake to cool before slicing.

6. Mango Coconut Panna Cotta Bliss

Description: Transport yourself to a tropical paradise with this velvety mango coconut panna cotta. A delicious and attractive dessert that's surprisingly easy to make.

Serving Size: 6 servings

Prep Time: 20 minutes

Setting Time: 4 hours (refrigeration) Ingredients:

1 cup mango puree

1 cup coconut milk

1/2 cup sugar

2 teaspoons gelatin

2 tablespoons water

Fresh mango slices for garnish

Instructions:

In a small bowl, sprinkle gelatin over water and let it bloom for 5 minutes.

In a saucepan, boil mango puree, coconut milk, and sugar until it just begins to simmer. Remove from heat.

Add the bloomed gelatin to the warm mango-coconut liquid, stirring until entirely dissolved.

Strain the mixture to ensure a smooth texture.

Pour the panna cotta mixture into serving glasses or molds.

Refrigerate for at least 4 hours or until set.

Garnish with fresh mango slices before serving.

7. Lemon Blueberry Mascarpone Tart

Description: A balanced blend of acidic lemon, sweet blueberries, and creamy mascarpone, this tart is a burst of summer sensations in every bite.

Serving Size: 8 slices

Prep Time: 30 minutes

Cooking Time: 25 minutes

Ingredients:

1 1/2 cups all-purpose flour

1/2 cup powdered sugar

1/2 cup unsalted butter, cold and cubed

8 ounces mascarpone cheese

1/2 cup sugar Zest and juice of 2 lemons

2 big eggs

1 cup fresh blueberries

Instructions:

Preheat the oven to 375°F (190°C) and grease a tart pan.

In a food processor, combine flour, powdered sugar, and cold cubed butter. Pulse until the mixture resembles coarse crumbs.

Press the crust mixture into the tart pan, covering the bottom and up the sides. Chill for 15 minutes.

In a bowl, mix mascarpone, sugar, lemon zest, and lemon juice until creamy. Add eggs one at a time, mixing well.

Pour the mascarpone filling into the cold crust.

Sprinkle fresh blueberries over the filling.

Bake for 25 minutes or until the filling is set and the crust is brown.

Allow the tart to cool before slicing.

8. Caramel Pecan Chocolate Chip Cookie Bars

Description: Experience the ultimate cookie bar delight with layers of gooey caramel, crunchy nuts, and rich chocolate chips. A lovely take on regular chocolate chip cookies.

Serving Size: 16 bars

Prep Time: 20 minutes

Cooking Time: 25 minutes

Ingredients:

2 1/4 cups all-purpose flour

1/2 teaspoon baking soda

1 cup unsalted butter, softened

1/2 cup granulated sugar

1 cup brown sugar, packed

2 big eggs

2 teaspoons vanilla extract

1 cup chocolate chips

1 cup chopped pecans

1 cup caramel sauce

Instructions: Preheat the oven to 350°F (175°C) and line a baking pan with parchment paper.

In a bowl, stir together flour and baking soda. Set aside.

In a large mixing basin, beat together melted butter, granulated sugar, and brown sugar until light and fluffy.

Add eggs one at a time, beating thoroughly after each addition. Stir in vanilla extract.

Gradually add the flour mixture to the wet ingredients, mixing until just mixed.

Fold in chocolate chips and chopped pecans.

Press half of the cookie batter into the prepared pan. Pour caramel sauce over the dough.

Drop spoonfuls of the leftover cookie dough on top of the caramel.

Bake for 25 minutes or until the edges are golden brown.

Allow to cool before cutting into bars.

9. Dark Chocolate Raspberry Truffle Cake Description: A sophisticated and delicious dark chocolate cake covered with velvety raspberry truffle filling. This dessert is a celebration of the timeless marriage of chocolate and raspberries.

Serving Size: 12 slices

Prep Time: 30 minutes

Cooking Time: 35 minutes

Ingredients:

1 3/4 cups all-purpose flour

1 1/2 tablespoons baking powder

1/2 teaspoon baking soda

1/2 cup unsweetened cocoa powder

1 1/2 cups granulated sugar

1/2 cup unsalted butter, softened

2 big eggs

1 teaspoon vanilla extract

1 cup buttermilk

8 ounces dark chocolate, chopped

1/2 cup thick cream

1 cup fresh raspberries

Instructions:

Preheat the oven to 350°F (175°C) and butter and flour two 9-inch cake pans.

In a bowl, whisk together flour, baking powder, baking soda, and cocoa powder. Set aside.

In a large mixing basin, beat together sugar and melted butter until light and fluffy.

Add eggs one at a time, beating thoroughly after each addition. Stir in vanilla extract.

Gradually add the dry components to the wet ingredients, alternating with buttermilk, beginning and finishing with the dry ingredients. Mix until just mixed.

Divide the batter between the prepared pans and smooth the tops.

Bake for 30-35 minutes or until a toothpick inserted into the center comes out clean.

While the cakes cool, make the raspberry truffle filling by melting dark chocolate with heavy cream. Allow it to cool.

Once the cakes are cool, place a layer of raspberry truffle filling on top of one cake layer. Place the second layer on top and ice the entire cake with the remaining filling.

Garnish with fresh raspberries.

10. Vanilla Bean Bourbon Creme Brulee

Description: Elevate the classic crème brulee with the warm aromas of vanilla bean and a dash of bourbon. This exquisite dessert is excellent for special occasions.

Serving Size: 6 servings

Prep Time: 20 minutes

Cooking Time: 45 minutes

Chilling Time: 4 hours

Ingredients:

2 cups heavy cream

1 vanilla bean, split, and seeds scraped

1/2 cup granulated sugar

4 big egg yolks

2 tablespoons bourbon

Brown sugar for caramelizing

Instructions:

Preheat the oven to 325°F (160°C) and set 6 ramekins in a baking dish.

In a saucepan, heat heavy cream and vanilla bean (seeds and pod) until it just begins to simmer. Remove from heat and let it soak for 15 minutes.

In a bowl, mix sugar and egg yolks until pale.

Gradually add the cream mixture to the egg mixture, whisking constantly.

Strain the custard to remove the vanilla bean pod.

Stir in bourbon.

Divide the custard among the ramekins.

Place the baking dish in the oven and pour hot water into the dish until it comes halfway up the edges of the ramekins.

Bake for 40-45 minutes or until the custard is firm but still a little jiggly in the center.

Chill the crème brulee in the refrigerator for at least 4 hours before dusting a thin coating of brown sugar on top and caramelizing with a kitchen torch.

Section 6: Appetizers

Title: Caprese Skewers Description: A delicious spin on the traditional Caprese salad.

Serving Size: 10 skewers

Prep Time: 15 minutes

Ingredients: Cherry tomatoes, fresh mozzarella balls, fresh basil leaves, balsamic glaze.

Instructions: Thread one tomato, one mozzarella ball, and one basil leaf onto each skewer. Drizzle with balsamic glaze before serving.

Title: Spinach and Artichoke Dip Description: Creamy and flavorful dip with a wonderful combination of spinach and artichokes.

Serving Size: 8 servings

Prep Time: 20 minutes

Ingredients: Frozen chopped spinach, artichoke hearts, cream cheese, sour cream, garlic, Parmesan cheese.

Instructions: Mix ingredients, bake until bubbling, then serve with tortilla chips or sliced baguette.

Title: filled Mushrooms Description: Elegant entrée with delicious filled mushrooms.

Serving Size: 12 mushrooms

Prep Time: 25 minutes

Ingredients: Mushrooms, cream cheese, garlic, breadcrumbs, Parmesan cheese, fresh herbs.

Instructions: Remove mushroom stems, combine filling, fill mushrooms, bake till brown.

Title: Shrimp Cocktail Description: Classic shrimp cocktail with a zesty homemade cocktail sauce.

Serving Size: 6 servings

Prep Time: 10 minutes

Ingredients: Cooked shrimp, ketchup, horseradish, lemon juice, Worcestershire sauce.

Instructions: Mix sauce ingredients, refrigerate, and serve with shrimp.

Title: Bruschetta with Tomato and Basil

Description: Refreshing bruschetta accentuating the tastes of juicy tomatoes and fresh basil.

Serving Size: 8 slices

Prep Time: 15 minutes

Ingredients: Baguette, tomatoes, fresh basil, garlic, olive oil, balsamic vinegar.

Instructions: Toast bread, rub with garlic, top with diced tomatoes and basil, sprinkle with olive oil and balsamic vinegar.

Title: Deviled Eggs

Description: Classic deviled eggs with a creamy and zesty filling.

Serving Size: 12 halves

Prep Time: 20 minutes

Ingredients: Hard-boiled eggs, mayonnaise, Dijon mustard, paprika.

Instructions: Cut eggs in half, combine yolks with mayo and mustard, put into egg whites, sprinkle with paprika.

Title: Chicken Satay Skewers Description: Grilled chicken skewers with a delicious peanut sauce.

Serving Size: 10 skewers

Prep Time: 30 minutes

Ingredients: Chicken strips, soy sauce, ginger, garlic, peanut butter, lime juice.

Instructions: Marinate chicken, thread onto skewers, cook, serve with peanut sauce.

Title: Avocado and Black Bean Salsa Description: Fresh salsa with creamy avocado and meaty black beans.

Serving Size: 6 servings

Prep Time: 15 minutes

Ingredients: Avocado, black beans, tomatoes, red onion, cilantro, lime juice.

Instructions: Dice items, combine gently, refrigerate, and serve with tortilla chips.

Title: Mini Quiches Description: Bite-sized quiches with a variety of ingredients.

Serving Size: 24 mini quiches

Prep Time: 25 minutes

Ingredients: Pie crust, eggs, milk, cheese, ham, spinach, mushrooms.

Instructions: Cut pie crust, put into small muffin pans, fill with ingredients, bake until set.

Title: Prosciutto-Wrapped Asparagus

Description: Elegant and tasty asparagus stalks covered with prosciutto.

Serving Size: 12 spears

Prep Time: 20 minutes

Ingredients: Asparagus, prosciutto, olive oil, black pepper.

Instructions: Wrap asparagus spears with prosciutto, spray with olive oil, bake until asparagus is soft.

Section 7: soups and salads

1. Chicken Noodle Soup Description: Classic comfort food with a twist.

Serving Size: 4

Prep Time: 15 minutes

Ingredients: 2 cups shredded cooked chicken 8 cups chicken broth

1 cup chopped carrots

1 cup diced celery

1 cup egg noodles

1 teaspoon dried thyme

Instructions: In a large saucepan, bring chicken stock to a boil.

Add carrots, celery, and thyme. Simmer until veggies are soft.

Stir in shredded chicken and egg noodles. Cook until the noodles are done.

Season with salt and pepper to taste.

2. Caprese Salad Description: A delicious Italian salad emphasizing tomatoes and mozzarella.

Serving Size: 2 Prep Time: 10 minutes

Ingredients: 2 big tomatoes, sliced 1 cup fresh mozzarella, sliced 1/4 cup fresh basil leaves

2 tablespoons balsamic glaze

Salt and pepper to taste

Instructions: Arrange tomato and mozzarella slices on a dish.

Tuck fresh basil leaves between slices.

Drizzle with balsamic glaze and season with salt and pepper.

3. Minestrone Soup Description: Hearty Italian vegetable soup.

Serving Size: 6

Prep Time: 20 minutes

Ingredients: 1 cup diced onion

1 cup chopped carrots

1 cup diced zucchini

1 cup diced potatoes

1 can (15 oz) chopped tomatoes

4 cups veggie broth 1 cup spaghetti shells

Instructions: Sauté onions until transparent, add carrots, zucchini, and potatoes.

Stir in chopped tomatoes and veggie broth. Simmer until veggies are soft.

Cook pasta separately and add to the soup before serving.

4. Greek Salad Description: A bright and lively salad with Mediterranean tastes.

Serving Size: 4 Prep Time: 15 minutes

Ingredients: 2 cups cherry tomatoes, halved 1 cucumber, diced 1 cup Kalamata olives, pitted 1 cup feta cheese, crumbled

1/4 cup red onion, thinly sliced

2 tablespoons olive oil

1 tablespoon red wine vinegar

Instructions:

Combine tomatoes, cucumber, olives, feta, and red onion in a bowl.

In a small bowl, mix olive oil and red wine vinegar.

Drizzle dressing over the salad and stir gently.

5. Butternut Squash Soup Description: Creamy and flavorful fall-inspired soup.

Serving Size: 4

Prep Time: 25 minutes

Ingredients: 1 medium butternut squash, peeled and cubed 1 onion, chopped 2 cloves garlic, minced

4 cups vegetable broth

1 teaspoon dried sage

Salt and pepper to taste

Instructions: Sauté onion and garlic until softened.

Add butternut squash, sage, and vegetable broth. Simmer until the squash is soft.

Blend until smooth. Season with salt and pepper.

6. Caesar Salad Description: Classic Caesar salad with homemade dressing.

Serving Size: 2 Prep Time: 15 minutes

Ingredients: 1 head romaine lettuce, chopped 1/2 cup croutons

1/4 cup grated Parmesan cheese

1/4 cup Caesar dressing

Instructions: Toss chopped lettuce with croutons and Parmesan.

Drizzle Caesar dressing over the salad and toss until covered.

7. Tomato Basil Soup

Description: Rich and savory tomato soup with a dash of basil.

Serving Size: 4

Prep Time: 20 minutes

Ingredients: 6 cups ripe tomatoes, chopped 1 onion, sliced

3 cloves garlic, minced

4 cups vegetable broth

1/2 cup fresh basil, chopped

Salt and pepper to taste

Instructions: Sauté onion and garlic until aromatic.

Add tomatoes, vegetable broth, and basil. Simmer until tomatoes are tender.

Blend until smooth. Season with salt and pepper.

8. Cobb Salad Description: A substantial salad with a blend of tastes and textures.

Serving Size: 2 Prep Time: 15 minutes

Ingredients: 2 cups mixed greens

1 cup cooked chicken, diced 1 avocado, sliced 1/2 cup cherry tomatoes, halved 1/4 cup blue cheese, crumbled 2 hard-boiled eggs, sliced 1/4 cup ranch dressing

Instructions: Arrange mixed greens on a platter.

Top with chicken, avocado, tomatoes, blue cheese, and eggs.

Drizzle with ranch dressing.

9. Mushroom Barley Soup Description: Hearty soup with earthy mushrooms and healthy barley.

Serving Size: 6 Prep Time: 30 minutes

Ingredients: 1 cup pearl barley

1 cup diced onion

2 cups sliced mushrooms

4 cups vegetable broth 2 carrots, diced

2 celery stalks, chopped

directions: Cook barley according to package directions.

Sauté onions and mushrooms until tender.

Add barley, vegetable broth, carrots, and celery. Simmer until veggies are soft.

10. Spinach Strawberry Salad Description: Light and refreshing salad with a fruity touch.

Serving Size: 4

Prep Time: 15 minutes Ingredients:

4 cups baby spinach

1 cup sliced strawberries

1/2 cup candied pecans

1/4 cup feta cheese, crumbled

Balsamic vinaigrette dressing

Instructions:

Combine spinach,

Section 8: Side dishes

1. Garlic Parmesan Roasted Brussels Sprouts Description:

A savory take on Brussels sprouts with crispy skin and a blast of garlic and Parmesan flavor.

Serving Size: 4

Prep Time: 10 minutes

Ingredients: 1 lb Brussels sprouts, halved

2 tbsp olive oil

3 cloves garlic, minced

1/4 cup grated Parmesan cheese

Salt and pepper to taste

Instructions:

Preheat oven to 400°F (200°C).

Toss Brussels sprouts with olive oil, garlic, Parmesan, salt, and pepper.

Spread on a baking sheet and roast for 20-25 minutes until golden brown.

2. Mashed Sweet Potatoes with Cinnamon Butter Description: Creamy sweet potatoes mashed to perfection, topped with a fragrant cinnamon-infused butter.

Serving Size: 6

Prep Time: 15 minutes

Ingredients: 4 huge sweet potatoes, peeled and cubed

1/2 cup unsalted butter

1 tsp ground cinnamon

Salt to taste

Instructions: Boil sweet potatoes until soft, then drain.

Mash sweet potatoes and blend with butter, cinnamon, and salt until smooth.

3. Quinoa and Vegetable Stir-Fry

Description: A healthful side dish containing quinoa, bright veggies, and a soy-ginger sauce.

Serving Size: 4 Prep Time: 20 minutes

Ingredients: 1 cup quinoa, cooked

2 cups mixed veggies (bell peppers, broccoli, carrots)

3 tbsp soy sauce

1 tbsp sesame oil

1 tbsp fresh ginger, minced

Instructions:

Sauté veggies in sesame oil until crisp-tender.

Add cooked quinoa, soy sauce, and ginger. Stir thoroughly and simmer for a further 3-4 minutes.

4. Balsamic Glazed Roasted Asparagus Description: Roasted asparagus spears covered with a sweet and tart balsamic sauce.

Serving Size: 4

Prep Time: 10 minutes

Ingredients: 1 pound asparagus, trimmed

2 tbsp olive oil

3 tbsp balsamic vinegar

Salt and pepper to taste

Instructions: Toss asparagus with olive oil, balsamic vinegar, salt, and pepper.

Roast in a preheated oven at 425°F (220°C) for 15-20 minutes.

5. Lemon Herb Quinoa Salad Description: A delicious quinoa salad with a zesty lemon dressing and a variety of fresh herbs.

Serving Size: 6

Prep Time: 15 minutes

Ingredients: 2 cups cooked quinoa

1/4 cup fresh parsley, chopped 2 tbsp fresh mint, chopped Zest and juice of 1 lemon

3 tbsp olive oil

Instructions: In a bowl, add quinoa, parsley, mint, lemon zest, lemon juice, and olive oil. Mix thoroughly.

6. Creamy Garlic Parmesan Polenta Description: Silky and creamy polenta laced with garlic and Parmesan, a delightful side dish.

Serving Size: 4 Prep Time: 20 minutes

Ingredients:

1 cup cornmeal

4 cups chicken or veggie broth

1/2 cup grated Parmesan cheese

3 cloves garlic, minced

Instructions:

Bring broth to a boil, gradually whisk in cornmeal, stirring continually.

Stir in Parmesan and garlic, simmering until creamy.

7. Honey-drizzled Carrots with Dill Description: Tender carrots drizzled in honey and garnished with fresh dill for a sweet and herbaceous taste.

Serving Size: 4

Prep Time: 15 minutes

Ingredients: 1 pound carrots, peeled and sliced

2 tbsp honey

2 tbsp butter

1 tbsp fresh dill, chopped

Instructions:

Boil or simmer carrots until soft.

In a pan, melt butter and honey. Add carrots and stir until covered. Sprinkle with dill.

8. Caprese Salad Skewers Description: A bite-sized delicacy containing cherry tomatoes, mozzarella, and basil topped with balsamic sauce.

Serving Size: 8 skewers

Prep Time: 15 minutes

Ingredients: 1-pint cherry tomatoes

8 ounce fresh mozzarella balls

Fresh basil leaves

Balsamic glaze for drizzling

Instructions: Thread a tomato, mozzarella ball, and basil leaf onto each skewer.

Arrange skewers on a plate and sprinkle with balsamic glaze.

9. Crispy Parmesan Zucchini Fries Description: Zucchini sticks covered with Parmesan and breadcrumbs, fried till golden and served with marinara sauce.

Serving Size: 4

Prep Time: 20 minutes

Ingredients: 2 big zucchinis, sliced into fry

1 cup breadcrumbs

1/2 cup grated Parmesan

2 eggs, beaten

Instructions:

Dip zucchini sticks in beaten eggs, then cover in a combination of breadcrumbs and Parmesan.

Bake in a preheated oven at 425°F (220°C) for 15-20 minutes.

10. Roasted Garlic and Rosemary Potatoes

Description: Crispy roasted potatoes blended with the tastes of garlic and rosemary.

Serving Size: 6

Prep Time: 15 minutes

Ingredients:

2 pounds young potatoes, halved 3 tbsp olive oil

4 cloves garlic, minced 2 tbsp fresh rosemary, chopped

Instructions:

Toss potatoes with olive oil, garlic, and rosemary.

Roast in a preheated oven at 400°F (200

Chapter 4: Mastering Ninja Air Fryer Techniques

Open the maximum capacity of your Ninja Air Fryer with our exhaustive manual for cutting-edge air-searing procedures. Raise your culinary abilities as we dig into a domain of accuracy and flavor upgrades.

High level Air Searing Tips and Deceives

Jump profound into the complexities of air searing as we disclose progressed tips and deceives. Find the craft of accomplishing the ideal freshness, dominating temperature control, and streamlining cook times. Lift your culinary manifestations with procedures that go past the nuts and bolts.

Idealizing Your Baking Abilities

Take your baking abilities higher than ever with the Ninja Air Fryer. Investigate a range of magnificent recipes, from debauched pastries to distinctive bread. Release the force of convection baking and witness the sorcery of even and predictable outcomes, guaranteeing each heated magnum opus is a victory.

Barbecuing and Simmering Like a Master

Transform your Ninja Air Fryer into a flexible barbecuing and cooking force to be reckoned with.

Reveal the key to accomplishing that ideal single and delicious dish. From flavorful meats to lively vegetables, become a culinary virtuoso by excelling at barbecuing and cooking with accuracy.

Drying out for Solid Eating

Set out on an excursion of solid eating with the drying-out capacities of your Ninja Air Fryer. Figure out how to protect flavors while making healthy bites. Find different organic products, vegetables, and more that can be changed into tasty, supplement stuffed treats for irreproachable guilty pleasure.

In Section 4, we give a complete guide to release the maximum capacity of your Ninja Air Fryer. Lift your cooking abilities and make culinary works of art with certainty as you explore progressed air searing, wonderful baking, master barbecuing, and well-being cognizant of getting dried out. Your Ninja Air Fryer isn't simply a kitchen machine - it's your pass to culinary greatness.

Chapter 5: Affordable Culinary Magic

In the domain of culinary investigation, Section 5 unfurls a depository of shrewdness, uncovering the key to excelling at Reasonable Culinary Wizardry. We should leave on an excursion where cleverness meets flavor, and spending plan cordial joy turns into a culinary song of devotion.

Spending plan Cordial Fixing Replacements

Open the speculative chemistry of replacement as we dive into shrewd options that won't burn through every last dollar. Find how basic trades can change customary recipes into unprecedented culinary manifestations. From storeroom staples to cunning fixing substitutions, this segment fills in as a culinary compass for those exploring the way of prudent yet delightful cooking.

Cash Saving Feast Arranging Procedures

In the ensemble of flavors, vital feast arranging becomes the overwhelming focus. Part 5 reveals a collection of savvy procedures to organize your week's menu. Figure out how to hit the dance floor with occasional produce, embrace clump cooking, and use extras as resources. This part is a plan for culinary effectiveness, guaranteeing that each penny spent converts into an ensemble of fulfilling dinners.

Frugal Ninja Air Fryer Hacks

Enter the domain of the Frugal Ninja, where the air fryer turns into a weapon of thrifty development. Reveal hacks and methods that lift your air-broiling game while watching out for your financial plan. From changing humble fixings into firm pleasures to boosting the capability of your air fryer, this segment engages you to employ kitchen devices like a carefully prepared culinary ninja.

As we explore the universe of Reasonable Culinary Enchantment, these experiences and techniques engage you to make culinary marvels without depleting your wallet. It's not just about cooking; it's tied in with changing humble fixings into an orchestra of flavors, each spending plans cordial show-stopper in turn. Prepared to set out on this gastronomic experience? Turn the page and let the enchantment unfurl.

Chapter 6: Culinary Wellness

Opening the Capability of Culinary Wellbeing: An Excursion into Nutritious and Careful Cooking

In Section 6, we dig into the domain of culinary health, investigating the extraordinary impacts of embracing careful cooking rehearses and outfitting the nourishing advantages of air searing with your Ninja Air Fryer.

Dietary Advantages of Air Searing

Find the culinary upheaval delivered via air searing as we unwind the nourishing advantages that make it a distinct advantage in the kitchen. From decreased oil utilization to safeguarding the normal integrity of fixings, air broiling takes care of taste buds as well as advances a well-being cognizant way of life. Figure out how this imaginative cooking strategy can lift your culinary experience while remembering your prosperity.

Good dieting Propensities with Your Ninja Air Fryer

Leave on a culinary experience with your Ninja Air Fryer as we guide you through the formation of delicious dishes that line up with smart dieting propensities. From fresh yet virtuous snacks to healthy fundamental courses, this segment gives pragmatic tips and recipes that grandstand the flexibility of your air fryer. Hoist your dietary admission without settling on flavor, and rethink how you approach smart dieting.

Careful Cooking for a Fair Way of Life

Culinary health reaches out past the fixings; it envelops the attitude with which we approach cooking. Plunge into the idea of careful cooking and its job in encouraging a decent way of life. Investigate how being available in the kitchen, picking quality fixings, and relishing each step of the cooking system add to general prosperity. This section is a manual for developing care through the demonstration of getting ready and appreciating supporting dinners.

As we leave on this culinary excursion, Part 6 intends to engage you with the information and abilities to embrace a comprehensive way to deal with cooking — one that entices your taste buds as well as sustains your body and soul. Lift your culinary ability, cultivate good dieting propensities, and leave on a way to a fair way of life with the extraordinary bits of knowledge looking for you in this section.

Chapter 7: Troubleshooting Guide

Embarking on your culinary journey with an air fryer is an exciting adventure, but even the most seasoned chefs encounter hiccups along the way. In this comprehensive Troubleshooting Guide, we delve into the most common air fryer mistakes and provide practical solutions to ensure your cooking endeavors are flawless.

Common Air Fryer Mistakes and Solutions

1. **Uneven Cooking:**

Mistake: Placing too much food in the basket.

Solution: Optimize airflow by arranging food in a single layer, ensuring each piece receives equal heat distribution.

2. **Food sticking to the basket:**

Mistake: Not preheating the air fryer or not using oil.

Solution: Preheat the appliance and lightly coat food with oil to prevent sticking, ensuring a crispy exterior.

3. **Rubbery Texture:**

Mistake: Overcrowding the basket.

Solution: Cook in batches to maintain optimal air circulation, preventing a soggy or rubbery texture.

4. **Smoke Production:**

Mistake: Using oils with low smoke points.

Solution: Choose oils with higher smoke points like avocado or grapeseed oil to avoid unwanted smoke during cooking.

FAQs – Addressing Your Culinary Concerns

Q1: Can I use parchment paper in my air fryer?

Answer: Yes, but trim it to fit the basket and avoid blocking the air vents to ensure proper circulation.

Q2: Why is my food not getting crispy?

Answer: Check if your food is properly dried before cooking and ensure it's not overcrowded in the basket for optimal crispiness.

Q3: How do I clean my air fryer?

Answer: Regularly clean the basket, tray, and interior with warm, soapy water, and refer to the manufacturer's instructions for specific care details.

Chapter 8: Community Delights

Set out on a culinary excursion like no other as we dive into the dynamic domain of Part 8: Local Area Joys. In this section, we not only enjoy the craft of sharing culinary manifestations yet in addition investigate the significant delight of associating with individual Ninja Air Fryer aficionados. Let the fragrance of fellowship swirl around as we find the force of online assets and networks committed to the specialty of air broiling.

Sharing Your Culinary Manifestations

Release your internal gourmet expert and feature your culinary ability as you jump into the wonderful experience of sharing your air-seared magnum opuses. Section 8 gives bits of knowledge into the specialty of the show, catching the pith of your manifestations through charming visuals, and connecting with stories. Raise your culinary excursion by interfacing with a worldwide crowd anxious to appreciate and be roused by your gastronomic undertakings.

Associating with Ninja Air Fryer Lovers

Find a local area of similar people energetic about the Ninja Air Fryer experience. Section 8 is your passage to framing associations, trading tips, and imparting stories to lovers who comprehend the subtleties of air broiling. Whether you're a beginner looking for direction or an old pro anxious to bestow insight, the local area anticipates improving your culinary experience.

Online Assets and Networks

Explore the computerized scene with certainty as we uncover a mother lode of online assets and networks devoted to the Ninja Air Fryer peculiarity. From recipe storehouses arranged by specialists to gatherings humming with conversations, Section 8 furnishes you with the apparatuses to remain educated and locked in. Uncover unexpected, yet invaluable treasures, learn new procedures, and remain on the front line of air-searing advancement.

Part 8: Local area Joys is more than a culinary investigation; it's a festival of shared encounters and aggregate enthusiasm. Join the development, enhance your culinary voice, and drench yourself in the unique universe of Ninja Air Fryer fans. Your culinary local area anticipates, prepared to enjoy the delight of shared delights!

Bonus Section: 30-Day Meal Plan

Day 1:

Breakfast: Cereal with berries and a sprinkle of chia seeds

Nibble: Greek yogurt with honey and almonds

Lunch: Barbecued chicken serving of mixed greens with blended greens and balsamic vinaigrette

Nibble: Apple cuts with peanut butter

Supper: Prepared salmon, quinoa, and steamed broccoli

Day 2:

Breakfast: Entire grain toast with avocado and poached eggs

Nibble: Curds with pineapple pieces

Lunch: Turkey and vegetable wrap with entire grain tortilla

Nibble: Carrot sticks with hummus

Supper: Pan-seared tofu with earthy-colored rice and blended vegetables

Day 3:

Breakfast: Smoothie with spinach, banana, and protein powder

Nibble: Small bunch of blended nuts

Lunch: Lentil soup and a side of entire-grain bread

Nibble: Orange cuts

Supper: Barbecued shrimp, quinoa, and simmered asparagus

Day 4:

Breakfast: Entire grain hotcakes with new berries and a bit of Greek yogurt

Nibble: Cut cucumber with tzatziki sauce

Lunch: Quinoa salad with cherry tomatoes, feta cheddar, and a lemon vinaigrette

Nibble: Modest bunch of grapes

Supper: Heated chicken bosom, yam wedges, and sautéed green beans

Day 5:

Breakfast: Fried eggs with spinach and entire-grain toast

Nibble: Blended organic product salad

Lunch: Entire grain pasta with marinara sauce, barbecued vegetables, and lean ground turkey

Nibble: Celery sticks with cream cheddar

Supper: Barbecued steak, quinoa, and a side of broiled Brussels sprouts

Day 6:

Breakfast: Smoothie bowl with banana, berries, and granola

Nibble: Yogurt parfait with layers of granola and cut strawberries

Lunch: Chickpea and vegetable pan-fried food with earthy-colored rice

Nibble: Pear cuts with cheddar

Supper: Prepared cod, wild rice, and steamed asparagus

Day 7:

Breakfast: Avocado toast with poached eggs and cherry tomatoes

Nibble: Trail blend in with nuts and dried natural products

Lunch: Spinach and feta stuffed chicken bosom, quinoa, and cooked yams

Nibble: Kiwi cuts

Supper: Vegan stew with dark beans, corn, and tomatoes

Day 8:

Breakfast: Entire grain waffles with cut strawberries and a sprinkle of maple syrup

Nibble: Curds with cut peaches

Lunch: Turkey and avocado wrap with entire grain tortilla

Nibble: Modest bunch of cherry tomatoes with mozzarella cheddar

Supper: Barbecued salmon, quinoa, and a side of simmered Brussels sprouts

Day 9:

Breakfast: Veggie omelet with mushrooms, chime peppers, and feta cheddar

Nibble: Apple cuts with almond spread

Lunch: Lentil and vegetable curry with earthy-colored rice

Nibble: Carrot and cucumber sticks with hummus

Supper: Prepared chicken thighs, yam pound, and steamed broccoli

Day 10:

Breakfast: Greek yogurt parfait with granola, banana cuts, and a shower of honey

Nibble: Blended nuts and dried natural product

Lunch: Entire grain pasta salad with cherry tomatoes, olives, and barbecued chicken

Nibble: Orange cuts

Supper: Quinoa-stuffed chime peppers with dark beans, corn, and salsa

Day 11:

Breakfast: Short-term oats with blended berries and a sprinkle of flaxseeds

Nibble: Banana with a small bunch of pecans

Lunch: Quinoa bowl with dark beans, corn, avocado, and a lime vinaigrette

Nibble: Celery sticks with peanut butter

Supper: Barbecued shrimp, earthy colored rice, and sautéed zucchini

Day 12:

Breakfast: Entire grain bagel with smoked salmon, cream cheddar, and escapades

Nibble: Greek yogurt with cut kiwi

Lunch: Chicken and vegetable sautéed food with broccoli, chime peppers, and soy sauce

Nibble: Mango cuts

Supper: Prepared cod, yam fries, and a side serving of mixed greens with blended greens

Day 13:

Breakfast: Fried eggs with spinach and feta cheddar, presented with entire-grain toast

Nibble: Small bunch of blueberries

Lunch: Turkey and quinoa stuffed chime peppers

Nibble: Cherry tomatoes with mozzarella and basil

Supper: Barbecued chicken bosom, quinoa, and cooked Brussels sprouts

Day 14:

Breakfast: Smoothie with banana, spinach, protein powder, and almond milk

Nibble: Trail blend in with almonds, raisins, and dull chocolate

Lunch: Lentil soup with a side of entire grain bread

Nibble: Orange cuts

Supper: Sautéed tofu with earthy-colored rice and blended vegetables

Go ahead and keep adjusting the arrangement given your inclinations and nourishing objectives.

Consistency and assortment are vital to keeping a solid and pleasant eating schedule. On the off chance that you have particular dietary prerequisites or well-being concerns, talk with a medical care proficient or an enrolled dietitian for customized guidance.

Day 15:

Breakfast: Acai bowl finished off with granola, cut banana, and coconut pieces

Nibble: Curds with pineapple lumps

Lunch: Entire grain wrap with barbecued chicken, lettuce, tomato, and tzatziki sauce

Nibble: Modest bunch of grapes

Supper: Heated salmon, quinoa, and steamed broccoli

Day 16:

Breakfast: Entire grain toast with crushed avocado and poached eggs

Nibble: Blended organic product salad

Lunch: Quinoa salad with cherry tomatoes, cucumber, feta cheddar, and balsamic vinaigrette

Nibble: Carrot sticks with hummus

Supper: Barbecued shrimp, earthy-colored rice, and simmered asparagus

Day 17:

Breakfast: Smoothie with spinach, banana, and protein powder

Nibble: Yogurt parfait with granola and cut strawberries

Lunch: Turkey and vegetable sautéed food with earthy-colored rice

Nibble: Pear cuts with cheddar

Supper: Prepared chicken bosom, yam wedges, and sautéed green beans

Day 18:

Breakfast: Fried eggs with spinach and entire grain toast

Nibble: Apple cuts with peanut butter

Lunch: Chickpea and vegetable wrap with entire grain tortilla

Nibble: Celery sticks with cream cheddar

Supper: Barbecued steak, quinoa, and a side of broiled Brussels sprouts

Day 19:

Breakfast: Entire grain flapjacks with new berries and a spot of Greek yogurt

Nibble: Cut cucumber with tzatziki sauce

Lunch: Lentil and vegetable curry with earthy-colored rice

Nibble: Small bunch of cherry tomatoes with mozzarella cheddar

Supper: Barbecued salmon, quinoa, and a side of cooked Brussels sprouts

Day 20:

Breakfast: Veggie omelet with mushrooms, ringer peppers, and feta cheddar

Nibble: Trail blend in with nuts and dried organic products

Lunch: Entire grain pasta with marinara sauce, barbecued vegetables, and lean ground turkey

Nibble: Orange cuts

Supper: Quinoa-stuffed chime peppers with dark beans, corn, and salsa

Day 21:

Breakfast: Greek yogurt parfait with granola, banana cuts, and a shower of honey

Nibble: Blended nuts and dried natural product

Lunch: Spinach and feta stuffed chicken bosom, quinoa, and cooked yams

Nibble: Kiwi cuts

Supper: Veggie lover stew with dark beans, corn, and tomatoes

Day 22:

Breakfast: Avocado toast with poached eggs and cherry tomatoes

Nibble: Small bunch of pecans with a banana

Lunch: Turkey and avocado wrap with entire grain tortilla

Nibble: Celery sticks with hummus

Supper: Heated cod, wild rice, and steamed asparagus

Day 23:

Breakfast: Short-term oats with blended berries and a sprinkle of flaxseeds

Nibble: Banana with a modest bunch of almonds

Lunch: Quinoa bowl with dark beans, corn, avocado, and a lime vinaigrette

Nibble: Celery sticks with peanut butter

Supper: Barbecued shrimp, earthy colored rice, and sautéed zucchini

Day 24:

Breakfast: Entire grain bagel with smoked salmon, cream cheddar, and escapades

Nibble: Greek yogurt with cut kiwi

Lunch: Chicken and vegetable pan-fried food with broccoli, ringer peppers, and soy sauce

Nibble: Mango cuts

Supper: Prepared chicken thighs, yam pound, and steamed broccoli

Day 25:

Breakfast: Acai bowl finished off with granola, cut banana, and coconut chips

Nibble: Curds with pineapple pieces

Lunch: Entire grain wrap with barbecued chicken, lettuce, tomato, and tzatziki sauce

Nibble: Small bunch of grapes

Supper: Prepared salmon, quinoa, and steamed broccoli

Day 26:

Breakfast: Entire grain toast with crushed avocado and poached eggs

Nibble: Blended natural product salad

Lunch: Quinoa salad with cherry tomatoes, cucumber, feta cheddar, and balsamic vinaigrette

Nibble: Carrot sticks with hummus

Supper: Barbecued shrimp, earthy-colored rice, and cooked asparagus

Day 27:

Breakfast: Smoothie with spinach, banana, and protein powder

Nibble: Yogurt parfait with granola and cut strawberries

Lunch: Turkey and vegetable pan-fried food with earthy-colored rice

Nibble: Pear cuts with cheddar

Supper: Heated chicken bosom, yam wedges, and sautéed green beans

Day 28:

Breakfast: Fried eggs with spinach and feta cheddar, presented with entire-grain toast

Nibble: Apple cuts with almond margarine

Lunch: Chickpea and vegetable wrap with entire grain tortilla

Nibble: Celery sticks with cream cheddar

Supper: Barbecued steak, quinoa, and a side of broiled Brussels sprouts

Day 29:

Breakfast: Entire grain flapjacks with new berries and a dab of Greek yogurt

Nibble: Cut cucumber with tzatziki sauce

Lunch: Lentil and vegetable curry with earthy-colored rice

Nibble: Small bunch of cherry tomatoes with mozzarella cheddar

Supper: Barbecued salmon, quinoa, and a side of cooked Brussels sprouts

Day 30:

Breakfast: Veggie omelet with mushrooms, chime peppers, and feta cheddar

Nibble: Trail blend in with nuts and dried natural products

Lunch: Entire grain pasta with marinara sauce, barbecued vegetables, and lean ground turkey

Nibble: Orange cuts

Supper: Quinoa-stuffed chime peppers with dark beans, corn, and salsa

List and Index

Improving Your Recipe Book

In a world immersed with culinary imagination, an efficient recipe book is a culinary friend that each home gourmet specialist wants. To hoist the client experience and smooth out the route, an exhaustive list and a beneficial supplement are fundamental parts.

File: Your Recipe Compass

The list fills in as a culinary compass, directing you quickly to the ideal recipe. A fastidiously created record classifies recipes in order, considering an easy route. Envision the simplicity of tracking down that wonderful treat or generous stew with only a look. Every passage gives the page number as well as important catchphrases, guaranteeing accuracy in your culinary investigation.

Helpful List for Speedy Recipe Reference

Our record is more than a simple rundown — it's a guide to culinary joy. From starters to sweets, the record offers a fast reference point for each desire. This easy understanding includes changing the recipe book into a unique device, saving time, and encouraging a pleasant cooking experience. The comfort of a very organized file isn't simply an extravagance; it's a need for any kitchen devotee.

Supplement: Uncovering Culinary Bits of Knowledge

Past the recipes lies a mother lode of culinary bits of knowledge. The supplement is a space saved for extra tips, graphs, and change tables — a culinary chronicle that improves your cooking process.

Extra Tips: Lifting Your Skill

Our recipe book goes past the nuts and bolts. The supplement incorporates extra tips and deceives to raise your culinary ability. From blade abilities to cutting-edge methods, these bits of knowledge give an establishment to development, transforming each home gourmet expert into a culinary virtuoso.

Outlines: Envisioning Culinary Authority

Visual students cheer! Our cautiously arranged graphs separate complex cooking processes into simple-to-follow visuals. Whether it's a heating-up temperature graph or a flavor matching aide, these diagrams change the opportunity for growth, making it open to gourmet experts of all expertise levels.

Change Tables: Accuracy in Each Action

In the realm of culinary imaginativeness, accuracy is central. The transformation tables in the reference section guarantee that your estimations are exact, whether you're managing ounces, grams, or cups. Not any more culinary mystery — simply immaculate execution.

All in all, our recipe book isn't simply an assortment of dishes; it's a thorough aid intended to improve your culinary excursion. The list and supplement work couple, giving a consistent and improving experience for each home cook. With this irreplaceable team, leave on a culinary experience where accuracy meets energy, and each dish is a work of art taking shape.

Conclusion

All in all, "The Ninja Air Fryer Pleasures Cookbook" fills in as a culinary aide, changing conventional cooking into a remarkable encounter. With a combination of development and flavor, this cookbook demystifies the craft of air searing as well as welcomes perusers to leave on a tasty excursion. From fresh hors d'oeuvres to tasty treats, the recipes inside these pages rethink what's conceivable with the Ninja Air Fryer. As perusers investigate the different exhibits of culinary manifestations, they are not simply following recipes; they are embracing a way of life that joins well-being, comfort, and, most importantly, taste. With each page turned, the cookbook rises above a simple assortment of recipes, turning into a friend in the kitchen — a wellspring of motivation and strengthening. Fundamentally, "Ninja Air Fryer Pleasures Cookbook" remains a demonstration of the culinary wonders reachable with the right machine and a sprinkle of inventiveness, moving prepares to hoist their feasts higher than ever.

This cookbook goes past being a simple gathering of recipes; a culinary experience urges perusers to explore different avenues regarding flavors and strategies. The careful guidelines and clear depictions not only make cooking available to all ability levels yet in addition welcome people to find the delight of creating café quality dishes in the solace of their homes. Via flawlessly mixing the proficiency of the Ninja Air Fryer with a different scope of fixings, this cookbook changes the conventional into the unprecedented, demonstrating that sound, delightful feasts can be easily accomplished. Fundamentally, "Ninja Air Fryer Enjoyments Cookbook" isn't simply a book about cooking; it's a tribute to the craft of relishing each nibble and savoring the course of creation in the core of one's kitchen.